# Patterns for InHABITing Success

Introduction by
**Dr. J.B. Hill**

Foreword and Compilation by
**Judith Williamson**

An Official Publication of
THE NAPOLEON HILL FOUNDATION

TO CLAIM YOUR ADDITIONAL FREE RESOURCES PLEASE VISIT
SOUNDWISDOM.COM/NAPHILL

© Copyright 2019—The Napoleon Hill Foundation

All rights reserved. This book is protected by the copyright laws of the United States of America. This book may not be copied or reprinted for commercial gain or profit. The use of short quotations or occasional page copying for personal or group study is permitted and encouraged. Permission will be granted upon request. For permissions requests, write to the publisher, addressed "Attention: Permissions Coordinator," at the address below.

SOUND WISDOM
P.O. Box 310
Shippensburg, PA 17257-0310

For more information on publishing and distribution rights, call 717-530-2122 or info@soundwisdom.com

Quantity Sales. Special discounts are available on quantity purchases by corporations, associations, and others. For details, contact the Sales Department at Sound Wisdom.

International rights inquiries please contact The Napoleon Hill Foundation at 276-328-6700 or email NapoleonHill@uvawise.edu

Reach us on the Internet: www.soundwisdom.com.

For Worldwide Distribution, Printed in the U.S.A.
Previous version published as ISBN: 978-1-937641-51-1
ISBN 13: 978-1-64095-128-0
Ebook ISBN: 978-1-64095-129-7

Publisher's Notes: Not all references to economy and conditions have been updated from original writing. We think you'll agree that the messages contained in this book are timeless.

While efforts have been made to verify information contained in this publication, neither the author nor the publisher assumes any responsibility for errors, inaccuracies, or omissions.

While this publication is chock-full of useful, practical information; it is not intended to be legal or accounting advice. All readers are advised to seek competent lawyers and accountants to follow laws and regulations that may apply to specific situations.

The reader of this publication assumes responsibility for the use of the information. The author and publisher assume no responsibility or liability whatsoever on the behalf of the reader of this publication.

1 2 3 4 5 6 7 8 9 / 23 22 21 20 19

Cover/Jacket designer Eileen Rockwell

# FOREWORD

Dear Readers,

Success remains a mystery for most people because neuroscience is not in their success vocabulary. This scientific side of success is founded in the belief that even though our conscious mind may be focused on the best possible success outcome, it is our enormous reservoir of programmed behaviors housed in our subconscious mind that either propels us onward toward fulfillment of our desires or terminates the program. For many people, this simple fact seems impossible and that is precisely why it is not considered in the outcome of our conscious desires.

In *The Biology of Belief*, Bruce H. Lipton, Ph.D., states: "The learned behaviors and beliefs acquired from other people, such as parents, peers, and teachers, may not support the goals of our conscious mind. The biggest impediments to realizing the successes of which we dream are the limitations programmed into the subconscious."

Dr. Lipton has hit the nail on the head with his assessment of the power of the subconscious mind in a person's daily life, however, he admits that beyond his extensive scientific findings relating to the life of cells and then extrapolated to the full blown functioning human, he is still uncertain as to how to best reprogram existing subconscious patterns. He adds: "As a preprogrammed behavior is unfolding, the observing conscious mind can step in, stop the behavior, and create a new response. Thus the conscious mind offers us free will, meaning we are not just victims of our programming. To pull that off however, you have to be fully conscious lest the programming take over, a difficult task, as anyone who's tried willpower can attest."

So, now that a major cause of failure is becoming increasingly apparent, how best does a person replace existing programs with new ones better suited for success? Books on self-improvement have suggested that first the "recording" be identified and next if it is an offending program, the "record" be mentally scratched and then consciously replaced with a new recording.

According to Dr. J. B. Hill, neuroplasticity in the human brain and nervous system allows for growth and development when new patterns of behavior are transplanted into existing programs. Therein is the panacea that Dr. Hill's grandfather, Napoleon Hill, discusses in the principle Cosmic Habitforce. The profound statement of belief that Dr. Napoleon Hill espouses,—"What the mind can conceive and believe, the mind can achieve."—is in fact rooted in neuroscience. Stated another way, it is now an established fact that conscious thought can determine predictable outcome as long as the conscious and subconscious mind are linked and the programs match.

In using a garden analogy, thoughts are seeds that are planted either intentionally or unintentionally in our minds. These seeds can be those healthy plants that are intended for harvest and consumption or they could be noxious plants that are injurious to our health and morals. Since only each of us is accountable for the one life we have been given, it becomes our job through the employment of free will to tend our interior space and extract the weeds that interfere with the best possible outcome for our garden.

Dr. Lipton states: "The subconscious mind's behaviors when we are not paying attention may not be our own creation because most of our fundamental behaviors were downloaded without question from observing other people." This fact is of great significance for two reasons: 1) we can modify behaviors that we no longer wish to express or manifest in our daily lives through free will, and 2) we can now recognize that we may be living vicariously someone else's life because we are following their downloads or programs. This can be the ultimate wake-up call for someone having difficulty in achieving the success that they desire in life.

And, here's the rest of the solution. Now that the cause is known, we can use existing material from the Masters of Habit Development that have been around for a long time. Perhaps, an amount of skepticism existed prior to understanding how the neurological system functions in the human. But now, Emile Coué, Napoleon Hill, Claude Bristol, Ben Sweetland, Ella Wheeler Wilcox, Florence Scovel Shinn and a host of others make perfect sense in the directives that they give for conditioning our outcomes by conditioning our subconscious mind for success.

Success is best understood as a series of related habits which are deliberate actions taken over time that because of repetition become rote. Once these success habits become rote they perform right on schedule for us because they have become a downloaded pattern housed in our subconscious mind. Once entrenched in our subconscious mind, these routine habits have the determination and persistence of weeds, but conversely these now deliberatively cultivated habits are higher functioning and productive. They are the children of our thoughts, and they are intentionally placed inside our inner psyche to produce offspring that complement who we are and what we still intend to become.

What more marvelous gift could anyone other than a benevolent God give to His children? Once the key is found to this Treasure Chest, all the goodness of the universe will be ours for the asking. The simple directive – Knock – Seek – Ask – has always been there for us!

  Be Your Very Best Always,
  Judy Williamson
  Director: Napoleon Hill World Learning Center,
  Purdue University Calumet

*Biology of Belief.* Bruce H. Lipton, Ph.D. Hay House, Inc. 2009. Pg. 139.

# CONTENTS

NAPOLEON HILL UNIVERSITY:
*Patterns for InHABITing Success*

Texts 1-14 are
Ben Sweetland's Magic Formula–
*A Course of Lessons Designed to Teach
you HOW to tap the POWERS of MIND*

Text No. 1: Determination .................... 25
   Pattern 1: A Practice – Emile Coué:
     How To Practice Conscious Autosuggestion .. 37
   Pattern 2: A Practice – Napoleon Hill:
     Self-Confidence Formula ................. 39

Text No. 2: You are a Mind with a Body ......... 43
   Pattern 3: A Suggestion – Dorothea Brande:
     Action for Success ...................... 53
   Pattern 4: A Practice – Claude Bristol:
     The Mirror Technique ................... 54

Text No. 3: Pictures are Patterns ................ 57
   Pattern 5: A Practice – Claude Bristol:
     Desire ................................. 66
   Pattern 6: A Practice – Napoleon Hill:
     Six Ways to turn Desires into Gold ......... 68

Text No. 4: The Magic Formula . . . . . . . . . . . . . . . . 71
   Pattern 7: A Meditation – Maltbie D. Babcock, D. D.:
   I Need Be No Failure! . . . . . . . . . . . . . . . . . . . 80
   Pattern 8: A Reading – Napoleon Hill:
   Self-Suggestion, the Connecting Link Between
   the Conscious and the Subconscious Mind . . . 81

Text No. 5: Physical Wellness and Tenseness . . . . . . 85
   Pattern 9: A Reading – Napoleon Hill: Habit . . . 95
   Pattern 10: A Suggestion – J. Martin Kohe:
   The Power to Choose . . . . . . . . . . . . . . . . . . . 98

Text No. 6: Self-Mastery . . . . . . . . . . . . . . . . . . . . . . 101
   Pattern 11: A Suggestion – Dorothy Carnegie:
   Five Big Ways to Rise above Disaster . . . . . . . 110
   Pattern 12: A Reading – Orison Swett Marden:
   Overcoming Environment . . . . . . . . . . . . . . . 110

Text No. 7: The Realm of Success . . . . . . . . . . . . . 113
   Pattern 13: A Practice – Napoleon Hill:
   The R2 A2 Formula: How to Recognize, Relate,
   Assimilate and Apply Success Principles . . . . . 122
   Pattern 14: A Suggestion – Erna Ferrell Grabe and Paul
   C. Ferrell: Success or Failure? You Decide . . . 125

Text No. 8: The Magic Wand . . . . . . . . . . . . . . . . . 127
   Pattern 15: A Reading – Emile Coué:
   Slaves of Suggestion . . . . . . . . . . . . . . . . . . . . 136
   Pattern 16: A Reading – Douglas Malloch: Habits 136

Text No. 9: Psychological Complexes . . . . . . . . . . . 139
   Pattern 17: A Reading – Florence Scovel Shinn:
   The Golden Nugget . . . . . . . . . . . . . . . . . . . . 149
   Pattern 18: A Suggestion – Ernest Holmes:
   Thought Patterns . . . . . . . . . . . . . . . . . . . . . . 150

**Text No. 10: Ideas – the Spark Plugs of Success** ... 153
   **Pattern 19:** A Reading – Walter Pitkin:
      The Value of Versatility ................ 162
   **Pattern 20:** A Meditation – Ben Sweetland:
      Your Life's Pattern .................... 163

**Text No. 11: Leadership** .................... 165
   **Pattern 21:** A Practice – Frederick Pierce:
      Dismiss the Rubbish .................. 174
   **Pattern 22:** A Reading – David Seabury:
      Habit Tendencies ..................... 176

**Text No. 12: Gaining a Good Memory** .......... 179
   **Pattern 23:** A Suggestion – W. Clement Stone:
      Do It Now! .......................... 188
   **Pattern 24:** A Meditation – Napoleon Hill:
      Habits of Growth .................... 189

**Text No. 13: Master of Your Own Destiny** ...... 193
   **Pattern 25:** A Practice – Claude Bristol and
      Harold Sherman: Fire of Enthusiasm ...... 202
   **Pattern 26:** A Suggestion – Claude Bristol and Harold
      Sherman: See Yourself As You Want To Be! ... 204

**Text No. 14: Course Overview and Summary** .... 207
   **Pattern 27:** A Reading – Ella Wheeler Wilcox:
      Discontent .......................... 217
   **Pattern 28:** A Meditation – Gospel of Matthew:
      Knock, Seek, Ask .................... 218

# INTRODUCTION
by Dr. J. B. Hill

*Every idea held in the mind through prolonged, concentrated thought takes on permanent form and continues to affect the bodily activity according to its nature, either consciously or unconsciously. Auto-suggestion which is nothing more or less than an idea held in the mind through thought, is the only known principle through which one may literally make himself over, after any pattern that he may choose.*

— NAPOLEON HILL

## NEUROPLASTICITY
### Another word for Cosmic Habit Force

According to the Holy Quran, Allah tells Adam and Eve <u>not to APPROACH</u> the tree of life.[1] Of course, this differs from the biblical version in which they are told <u>not to EAT</u> from the tree.[2] Another difference is that

---

[1] "O Adam! Dwell thou and thy wife in the Garden, and enjoy (its good things) as ye wish: but approach not this tree, or ye run into harm and transgression."

[2] And the LORD God commanded the man, saying, Of every tree of the garden thou mayest freely eat: But of the tree of the knowledge of good and evil, thou shalt not eat of it: for in the day that thou eatest there of thou shalt why surely die.

according to the Holy Quran, Satan tempts both Adam and Eve who then approach the forbidden tree together, but in the biblical version, Satan first tempts Eve into eating and then it is Eve who gets Adam to eat the forbidden fruit.

Now, what is clear from both versions is that at creation mankind was given three incredible gifts: human life itself with an immortal soul, the Garden of Eden and Free Will. Well, man lost Eden but he was left with the other two gifts—life and Free Will. But without Eden, the means to continue life was left to man to figure out for himself.

To accomplish this, man still had Free Will, giving him the ability to choose. It seems to me that Free Will, given to man at creation as a gift from God, must be incredibly important. I believe Free Will is one of the unnamed riches of life...and that it is the most important one. We <u>are</u> free ... to make choices: We choose to hate or we don't; we choose to love or we don't; we choose to believe ....or we don't; and we choose to succeed ...... or we don't.

With free will, we have the power to create an Eden for ourselves and for our family on Earth. However, most of us fail to achieve a new Eden here on earth. We tend to drift along, making decisions but only when we are forced to make them. WHY? We do this because it is safe and we are afraid of change. We would rather drift through life.

## INTRODUCTION

Napoleon Hill believed that drifting is the greatest reason for failure in life. In fact, he lists DRIFTING first and foremost among his 54 reasons for failure.[3] He wrote that it .... is just easier to "follow the course of least resistance, to go with the flow, to drift with the current with no particular destination in mind."

I have been guilty of it myself. I drifted in spite of being Napoleon Hill's grandson. And I drifted in spite of being able to bear witness to the truth of his words. I drifted for 25 years because I possessed job security. I was reasonably well paid. I felt good about myself. I drifted because I had no reason to change. But most of all, I drifted because I had no long term goals, no burning desire.

Phil Taylor[4] once told me that motivation starts somewhere between inspiration and desperation. He was exactly right in my case. Now, this does not mean that I had forgotten all of my dreams during those 25 years of drifting. I still had dreams, all right, but I had traded any hope for achieving them for job security.

For me, drifting felt like "waiting"—waiting for something to happen. Drifting leads to an unplanned future with only the certainty of an unexpected and premature old age. The planned future requires thought. But drifting is just the symptom that stems from the real problem that we all face—controlling our mind.

---

3 People drift through life when they don't have a goal, when they lose their focus toward that goal or when fear takes control of their mind.
4 Phil Taylor is an author and popular talk show host.

When we form a thought, brain cells called neurons will fire. Holding a thought will cause these neurons to recruit other neurons into a network. When you drop that thought the network unravels until the thought becomes a memory. Repetitively thinking the same thought, however, reinforces that memory to build a stronger network and one that is able to retain its structure until needed.

In effect, the brain rewires itself to facilitate thinking a certain thought ... this is an example of what neuroscientists call neuroplasticity. Remember that word: neuroplasticity—the mind's ability to rewire the brain.

Researchers have learned that thought is the agent that can be used to direct the brain and its subconscious. Physicians use cognitive therapy to overcome fear, promote health, reduce pain, AND even to elevate mood.

Some drug therapies will do this as well but unlike drug therapy, cognitive therapy can be permanent. The new understanding of the brain shows that the front of the brain (called the frontal cortex and the pre-frontal cortex) can re-organize the whole brain. The key is focused thought which provides us with the means to rewire our brain to achieve a goal—any goal.[5]

Today, when healthy eating has become almost vogue, it is popular to say that "we are what we eat." But science is also telling us that "we become what we think." For example, Tibetan monks meditate for several hours each

---

[5] Napoleon Hill said the same thing when he wrote about using the conscious mind to enlist the sub-conscious mind as an ally to achieve success in Chapter 12 of *Think and Grow Rich*.

day. The Dalai Lama sent 10 of these monks to the United States to participate in brain mapping studies. Their brains were studied during meditation and the part of brain involved in mood, depression, joy, and personality was very active while they meditated. Furthermore, that same area of the brain remained active for long periods after meditation. These areas are rarely as active, in people who do not meditate or do not pray.

The monks meditate to achieve inner peace and tranquility and we now know that the process of meditation builds the neuronal networks that make this possible. Although Siddhārtha Gautama Buddha's "path of tranquility" is thought of as a spiritual path of awakening, it is never the less real and available to all of us to some extent without the need for religious association.

Nuns from the Franciscan Order care for the poor, the sick, the orphaned, and the dying and they pray 5 times a day. During prayers, the part of their brain involving empathy has been studied and was found to be very active. The nuns leave prayer pious, joyful, and rededicated to caring for the helpless.

World famous mathematicians and taxi drivers have something in common[6]. They spend a large amount of time using the spatial relations part of the brain called the hippocampus. The hippocampus of these people demonstrates high levels of activity even after they are through work for the day.

Try getting to sleep after a couple hours playing chess;

---

6 *Buddha's Brain* by Rick Hanson, Ph.D.

your mind will be so energized that you cannot sleep. That is your hippocampus at work, unable to set aside the problems of chess. Can your mind do more with thought? Yes, much more!

**Success through a Positive Mental Attitude** is a landmark work written by Napoleon Hill and W. Clement Stone. The book is so well known that its title is almost a cliché and every serious modern success writer stresses the need for "positive thinking." Even Mark Victor Hansen uses "Positive Thinking" in the title of his new book.[7] Now, Deepak Chopra recently pointed out that negative thinking can also be useful. In fact, negative thinking is essential for framing a problem to find its solution. It is how we identify the tasks that we need to accomplish.

But what is the value of positive thinking? Well, positive thinking is used to overcome fear, gain confidence, and stimulates action toward a goal—all powerful reasons for encouraging positive thinking. Recently, several medical journal articles [Subramanian, et all] have reported that a positive mood will enhance overall problem solving ability and, in particular, increase the use of insight to solve problems.[8] So, Positive Thinking actually makes us smarter!

Thinking about something frequently CAUSES us to think about it more often until it becomes a habit. It is up to

---

[7] *Chicken Soup for the Soul*: Think Positive: 101 Inspirational Stories about Counting Your Blessings and Having a Positive Attitude.

[8] "*A brain mechanism for facilitation of insight by positive affect*;" Karuna Subramaniam, John Kounios, Todd B. Parrish, and Mark Jung-Beeman; Journal of Neuro-Science.

us to decide if we want our thought habits to be negative or to be positive....this is the basis of cognitive therapy.

Other studies show that focused, planned, repetitive thinking can be used to overcome depression and even fear. This is accomplished by building new thought networks that are strengthened with positive input while weakening old thought networks by avoiding negative input. So the mind can form new neuronal networks. These networks help us accomplish tasks and they can help us succeed by turning the accomplishment of our goals into the "burning desire" that Napoleon Hill wrote about.

The area of the brain controlling the fingers of the left hand of a violinist demonstrates high activity during violin practice. However, the same area of the brain demonstrates high activity when a well-trained violinist simply imagines himself playing a particular score.

Professional golfers spend thousands of hours practicing. This collates the neurons that control the physical body into the networks that are needed to play golf well. Why do golfers visualize golf shots before attempting them? The process of visualizing a golf shot activates these networks so that they are available when needed.

Have you ever wondered why all diets CAN work but all diets FAIL? The reason why is that weight loss is NOT about the diet. Weight loss is about, well ... *life style changes* and everyone knows it.....Right?

Then why hasn't anyone published a weight loss book

that explains HOW to make those life style changes. Weight loss is not about the diet, that's just a tool. And it is not about diet tricks like keeping a food diary, planned shopping, etc.—those too are just tools.

In order to lose weight and keep it off permanently, the goal of weight loss must be transformed into a burning desire that is maintained by habit force like any other goal.[9] People who keep weight off for years do not develop heightened self-discipline; they simply learn not to crave the foods they once wanted.

So what do professional violinists, golfers, and successful dieters have in common? Each of them uses the conscious mind to rewire the brain to build networks that create a <u>force of habit</u> that cannot be denied or deterred.[10]

Although new findings in neuropsychology are exciting and have led to a score of how-to books, the common element to all of them is the need for a focused, repetitive effort to discipline our thoughts. The most astounding thing to me is that from a practical application perspective, nothing is new. Napoleon Hill figured it out 75 years ago. Napoleon Hill wrote that 6 steps are needed to accomplish a goal, any goal.

The first five steps provide a systematic method for understanding your goal, the price you must pay for it, and what you will have to do to achieve it. Dr. Hill wrote:

---

[9] Achieving this means integrating Napoleon Hill's six steps for achieving a goal with a coherent weight loss plan.

[10] This is the basis for Napoleon Hill's most famous saying, "What the mind can conceive and believe, the mind can achieve."

1. Fix in your mind exactly what you want to achieve—something specific.
2. Determine exactly what you must give in return to achieve your goal.
3. Establish a definite date by which you intend to achieve your goal.
4. Create a definite plan and begin at once, whether you are ready or not, to put this plan into action.
5. Write out a clear, concise statement of your goal, the time limit for its acquisition, what you intend to give in return for your goal, and the plan through which you intend to achieve it.

Napoleon Hill wrote, "The subconscious mind may be voluntarily directed *only through habit*." I am astounded by how correct he was. His 6th step was designed to activate the habit force required to achieve any goal. He wrote:

6. Read your written statement aloud, twice daily, once just before retiring at night, and once after arising in the morning.

He goes on to say that you must visualize and feel as if you have already achieved your goal. Let me give you an example of someone using these 6 steps.

A few years ago, I was at a local hospital seeing patients in the intensive care unit. A young, female physical therapist came in to the ICU and started talking with the unit secretary. I heard the secretary say, "How long have you been selling Mary Kay?" The physical therapist responded, "About 6 months."

Astounded, the secretary said, "Six months! That's all? How can you earn a new car in six months?" At this point, I couldn't help myself ... (I am, after all, who I am) ...I put my pen down and I interrupted, "I know how she did it."

They both looked at me. So I continued: "Every night when you get home from work, you review your goals and cross things off your "to-do" list. You then think about what you accomplished that day, set new intermediate goals, and make a to-do list for the next day."

The physical therapist looked at me, and with a questioning voice said, "EXACTLY." I answered, "Napoleon Hill"; she laughed, nodded, and replied *Think and Grow Rich!*

As I turned back to my note, I heard the secretary ask the therapist if she planned to sell Mary Kay products full time. The therapist answered, "Yes" and went on to say that she was on track to quit her work as a physical therapist in another year. She said that she dreamed about the day she would be able to do that.

If we look at her story, we see neuroplasticity at work. The therapist is focusing her thoughts towards her goal and building the neuronal networks necessary for her to achieve it by means of focused, repetitive thinking that will create a habit force in her.

But Napoleon Hill's six steps are there as well.

Napoleon Hill's 6 steps work because they employ neuroplasticity to take control of the mind by means of "mind discipline."

He wrote: "Men search all their lives for power and fame without attaining either, because they do not recognize that the real source of both is within their own minds."... "The mind that is properly disciplined and directed to definite ends is an irresistible power that recognizes no such reality as permanent defeat." ... "And the man that masters himself through self-discipline can never be mastered by others."... "It (mind discipline) is the sole means by which the mind can focus itself upon a definite major purpose until the power of habit force takes over."[11]

So, Napoleon Hill told us to use thought to take control of our mind and make use of Cosmic Habit Force, his term for what we now call neuroplasticity. It provides the means by which we can create our own Eden here on earth.

It took more than 75 years, but science is telling us to do exactly the same thing. Isn't it time to listen?

— JB Hill

---

11 *Master Key to Riches*, pg. 239.

# Magic Formula

*A new approach to the study of Creative Psychology which enables the student to make rapid strides toward self improvement*

By
## Ben Sweetland
Radio's Consulting Psychologist

---

Ben Sweetland is the contributing author to TEXTS 1-14 that appear in *Patterns for InHABITing Success*. Originally, these were printed as a small booklet in the 1950's entitled **Magic Formula**.

During his heyday, Ben Sweetland was a consulting psychologist who was broadcast on radio. He authored the motivational books entitled *I WILL* and *I CAN* as well as a syndicated column named "The Marriage Clinic."

As a popular lecturer, Sweetland stated that "95% of all human problems stem from a negative mind." It was his goal to educate his audience on the control of the subconscious mind.

Today, his techniques not only instruct the reader but place practice before theory. In the *Magic Formula* the author begins **Text 1** by telling readers that they will get immediate results. For Sweetland, the important aspect is to demonstrate that you can and will get immediate results! Try it and see for yourself!

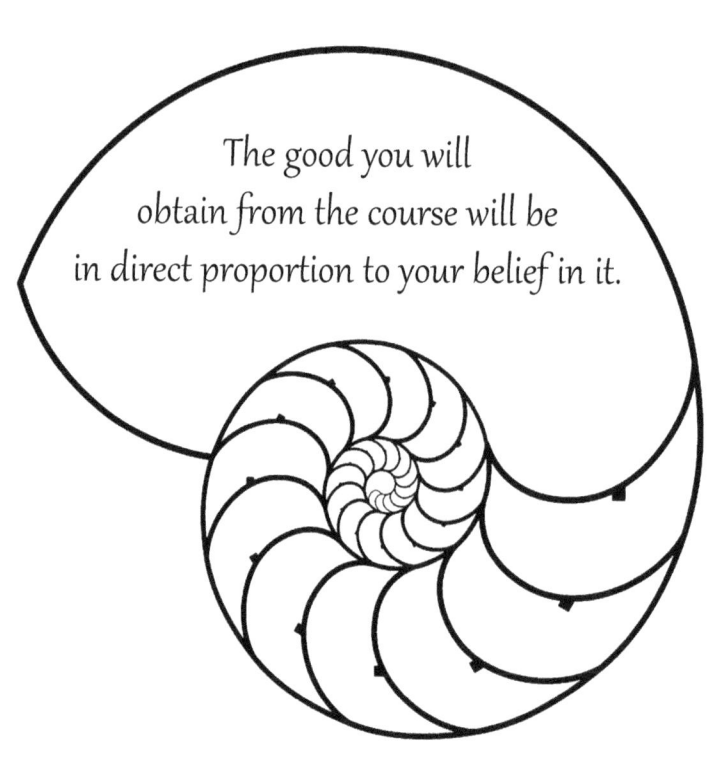

The good you will
obtain from the course will be
in direct proportion to your belief in it.

# TEXT No. 1

# DETERMINATION

SINCE the Magic Formula is unusual, I will start the very first text by being unusual; best described by the old adage: **putting the cart before the horse.** Yes, this is literally what I will do. It is common practice, in any form of instruction to begin by first explaining the principles, followed by application of the principles. Of course, this method is not without merit. You are taught why you do certain things before you learn how to do them.

You are taking this course for only **one** reason and that is to **get** results. Right? Well, wouldn't it be fine if we could start getting them from this first text onward,—instead of wading through several preliminary lessons before we begin to learn the application of the principles?

There would be very few television receivers purchased if it were necessary to complete a course of study in electronics before attempting to turn the knob which brings in the picture; yet, the layman would be astonished if he knew the forces he plays with when he does turn the television knob.

I can think of only one drawback in connection with the **immediate-action** plan I am adopting. The skeptical one might have difficulty in believing that the simple principles outlined could possibly be effective. But I'll risk this possibility in favor of those who want to see things happen **right now**. And, if the skeptics will lay aside their doubts for just one week and follow the suggestions given; their skepticism will be replaced with enthusiasm.

I am not belittling the individual who is skeptical. In this day and age we have become so accustomed to the careless manner in which promises are made, it does tax our credulity when we hear promises such as I have made in connection with the **Magic Formula**.

Perhaps it might be a happy thought if you were to adopt the "show me" attitude which is linked to the state of Missouri. Just declare to yourself that you will faithfully follow the rules laid down—and "it's just gotta be good."

All right. Now that we understand each other, let's go to work. Seven definite steps will be outlined in this text, each one unusually simple, but highly effective. And, since they are all inter-related, do not neglect any one of them.

My suggestion is that you read a step and then pause and think about it before going on to the next. Perhaps it would be wise to re-read it. Then begin using it. Make it a part of your life. And,—before starting on step number 1—make certain you are in a position to give it your undivided attention. If you have anything at all on your mind;—some task you should perform, **do it**, so that your mind will not be flitting from one thing to another. Be comfortable. Sit in a chair you like and have it placed where the light is good. And, by all means have a sharp pencil handy and **do not be afraid to make notes.** Wide margins have been provided for this purpose, be sure to use them.

Now then—are you ready?

**STEP 1.** Why are you taking this course? For self-improvement, of course. You want to make a success of your life. And, in using the word success, you mean it in its broadest form; success with your job or business; success in your home; success in building a powerful personality; success in gaining and retaining perfect health.

All right,—after you have achieved this success, it will **not** be something you bought. It will **not** be something I wrapped up in a package and delivered to you like a pound of sausage. **Success will be yours because you developed it.** You, yourself, did the things necessary to attract success to you. As a matter of fact, that is the only way you would want it. If success could be acquired from the shelves of stores, it would mean little or nothing to us. The hobbiest takes up the making of certain things for the thrill of creating something which did not exist before. With the completion of a project, he has built himself into it. It becomes a part of him.

Success **will** be yours, and it will be, because it is going to be of **your own making**. This leads us to the first step we will take;—and that is **Determination** to make this course the biggest thing you have ever done. Don't get frightened. This does not mean you are letting yourself in for a tedious grind of hard work. To the contrary you will feel that you are starting on the most exciting journey of your life. Have you ever worked a jig saw puzzle? At first you view a mass of irregular shaped pieces which do look confusing,—but you are determined to put the picture together. You look over the many segments, and each time you spot a piece which will fit into your picture, a sense of joy overtakes you. The moment you declare definitely to yourself that you will leave no stone unturned in gaining the maximum amount of good from this course, you will look at every phase of life as an interesting experience. And, as you receive the key to each of life's problems, you will discover life to be more fascinating than any game you could imagine.

So, before proceeding to the next step, pause and reflect over this one. Just realize that you have never been more determined regarding anything in your whole life. I told you that you would gain results immediately. If you stopped right now and had followed this one step literally, the good you would get would be worth hundreds of times what you have paid for the course,—yet you're just starting. In the final analysis—people who are successful **are so because they determined to be successful.**

**STEP 2.** You have determined to be a success! You now look around contemplating the first thing you should do in the direction of your goal. If a carpenter were given a building job,—and before him was his chest of tools, he would know, without doubt or hesitation, that he had before him the implements which would enable him to carry his assignment through to completion. This is the attitude I want you to take with reference to this MAGIC FORMULA. I want you to know—without doubt—you have that which is necessary for success and happiness. The good you will obtain from the course will be in direct proportion to your belief in it. If you approach each text with doubt—you may get some good, but nothing compared to what you can otherwise obtain. So far you have observed, I am sure, that every statement made is intended to appeal to your reasoning. It will continue that way throughout every phase of it. So, as the second step—gain the consciousness that you now have the key which will unlock the door to riches. This—with the determination you have acquired—will enable you to get on your way—**right now!**

**STEP 3.** If you do not already know it, before you

finish this course, you will have learned that all of our actions are controlled by our thoughts;—mind over matter, if you wish to express it that way. And, to the reasoning mind, this makes sense. You do not do something and later decide to do it,—do you? No, the deciding or thinking comes first.

Adhering to the statement made in the beginning, to the effect that we would start with the **application of principles** instead of the **explanation** of them, I will now tell you what I want you to do regarding your thinking—and in a later text will tell you why. Remember we are working on a **result-now** basis. Therefore, here is the third step. Repeat the following to yourself—slowly and thoughtfully.

> *"From this moment onward I will control my thoughts. I will guard against thoughts associated with failure, sorrow, gloom, poverty, illness, etc. I will avoid conversation dealing with subjects of a negative or discouraging nature. I will help others, so far as I can, to gain a positive state of mind, knowing that this will force me to set a good example which, in turn will prove of definite aid to me."*

It would be advisable to read this over two or three times. And, before going forward to the next step, think about this one for a few moments, then mentally review all three steps taken so far.

Don't you feel good already? Can't you sense a thrilling experience about to be yours? To speak broadly, can't you really feel you are entering into a new and glorious life?

**STEP 4.** For a moment, just imagine the one who has never travelled, who has never stepped foot outside of the community in which he lives. He has become quite discouraged seeing nothing but the same houses, the same faces—the same activities. Suddenly he has the opportunity to take an extended trip; a trip which will provide him with wonderful experiences, and, of course, all travel will be first class, and he will live only at the best resorts and hotels. His present state of boredom leaves him instantly. Instead of being unhappy over his present lot, his mind is dwelling on the joys to be experienced in the near future.

This is the feeling I want you to acquire regarding your circumstances as they are at the present. Instead of maintaining any feeling of **self-pity**, concentrate your thoughts on the new and glorious future which is **now** in the making.

In fact, the more humble your circumstances are now, the greater the happiness which is in store for you, due to the contrast.

So the essence of **STEP 4** is that you will accept—

gratefully—your present circumstances **no matter what they are**—as the ideal foundation on which to build.

**STEP 5.** This is the step which will require a bit of self discipline in order to refrain from being skeptical,—but remember, you have promised yourself not to be. I want you to begin day dreaming. Yes, I mean just that. I want you to begin picturing the kind of a life you would like to have. You have accepted the thought that you are now starting on an exciting journey, but where? That's a good question. One should know where he is going. And, it is not practical for me to make suggestions for you, because no two students would have the same objectives in life,—you agree, I'm sure!

You have learned that all action is preceded by thought. The man who has gone places is the one who originally visualized himself going to such places. Call it day dreaming, if you wish, but let me tell you at this point that there are two kinds of day dreaming; that which is backed by action and the one which fades out into nothingness. But, you're safe in day dreaming,—because in **STEP 2** you resolved through **determination** to make this step the most important one of your life;—so, with such a resolution, your day dreaming will be backed with definite action.

Therefore, visualize the life you have ahead of you as you would want it. Think of the material things you really want; money, home, car, clothes, etc. Picture the kind of a job or the kind of business you would like to have. Think of the changes you would like to make in your physical being such as **better health, mastering habit, overcoming timidity,** complexes and phobias. Visualize this new life,—not in the sense that you are wishing for these changes, but that you are **actually seeing** things—mentally—which are coming into your life. Yes, this step is the first one toward manifestation and, in later texts, you will learn **why** you attract these things to you.

I might urge you to keep your sights high. In manifestation, you will never rise above your consciousness. If you think in terms of little things, that is **all** you will ever get.

At this point, it might be well to again review **Step 2**, which relates to your determination. You can now ask yourself: "Just how strong is my determination?" If you can back the mental pictures you have with an invincible **determination,** nothing at all can hold you back. The sky, figuratively speaking, is your only limit.

**STEP 6.** This step will require an entire week. It, however, will be a glorious week. After you finish with this step—and the last one which follows; lay the text aside for the rest of the day. Do not read it again today,—but reflect over what you have read. Recall to mind, so far as possible, all of the seven steps given—and particularly their significance. Tomorrow, I want you to get your text and review Step 1 **only.** Think of it during the day—

and do so with a feeling of great happiness.

The next day, re-read Step 1 and also Step 2, and spend the rest of the day **applying** the thoughts which they contain. On the third day, review Steps 1, 2, and 3,—and keep those in mind throughout the day. On each successive day, start with Step 1 and go on through adding one more step, until you reach the day where you will have reviewed all seven steps. This will consume a week and by that time you will have laid such a foundation for this course, it will be impossible for you to see anything except a thrilling life ahead of you.

As you review each step, ask yourself the question: "Have I lived up to that one?" If there should be any doubt at all regarding this, review the doubtful step again and again until all doubt has disappeared.

STEP 7. Nothing stands still. It either moves forward or backward. This being true, each time you permit a day to pass without making some progress, you are slipping. So let this final step be your resolution to refuse to allow a day to pass without showing progress. Even a little motion is better than none at all,—so as the day comes to a close, be sure you can look back over some progress.

The motto: "Every Day I'm On My Way" is one which I want to have great significance for you. Frame it and place it on the wall in your breakfast room so that it will be present as a friendly reminder as you start your day. Let it remind you of the steps you will take during the day toward self improvement. Each time you do something which pleases you, with a feeling of joy, repeat to yourself: "Every Day I'm On My Way." And, you'll really mean it!

Need I ask if the promise contained in the first few lines of this text has been kept? You were told that we would start by getting results from the very beginning by working with the principles first and learning reasons later.

If you have taken the text seriously, and I'm sure you have, you have already gained immeasurably from what you have read. Success is nothing but an **attitude**—a state of mind. The man who achieves **Success** is the one who first thought in terms of success. Already you have gained a success attitude. You're beginning to see yourself as a success and you'll find that from this time onward—things will begin to happen—in your favor.

I hope I have not conveyed the impression that through the use of the **Magic Formula** you need only to move your finger and big things happen. You'll work for everything you'll ever get in this life, and it's a blessing that this is true. You'll work whether you are a success or not—and as you climb higher and higher toward success, you will discover that you work less in gaining an outstanding success than you do in being a failure.

Work can be pleasant or unpleasant, according to our attitude toward it.—We work hard—and **enjoy** it—when we work with a hobby. We work hard, and become greatly **fatigued**, when we do something unprofitable or unpleasant.

So, dear student,—this course will not take away the necessity of work;—but from now on everything you do will make you happy because you know it is a step toward your objective. It will be **progressive**.

By now, you are probably more enthusiastic than you have been for a long, long time. You have found, at last, a plan for successful living which you can accept; which appeals to your reasoning. Probably, with your enthusiasm, you feel almost like shouting these truths from the house tops—so that all may benefit from them. This is wonderful, and indicates that you will gain the maximum amount of good from the **Magic Formula**. But, in the beginning, at least, I would suggest that you refrain from discussing the principles with anyone except those who might be sympathetic with you. Those unfamiliar with the great powers of mind can be most critical of anyone who does endeavor to improve himself through an understanding of Creative Psychology. If you are fortunate enough to live with someone who is likewise eager for self improvement—then both of you would gain through discussing the various steps.

Now you have text one—and if you gained no more than you have up to this moment, I am sure you would feel it to be one of the best investments you have ever made.—But, you are just starting. Each subsequent text will open new realms of happiness for you. Don't get too anxious regarding future subjects. They will take care of themselves. The more thoroughly you master each passing monograph, the more good you'll get from it.

And, as for many years I have always ended my radio broadcasts: -

May Joy and Peace Be Yours

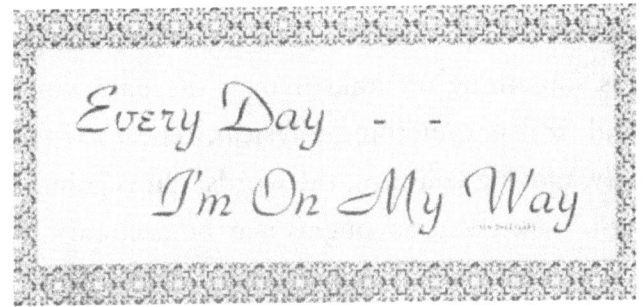

## InHABITing Pattern #1: A Practice
*How To Practice Conscious Autosuggestion*
by Emile Coué

Every morning before getting up and every evening as soon as you are in bed, shut your eyes, and repeat twenty times in succession, *moving your lips* (this is indispensable), and counting *mechanically* on a long string with twenty knots, the following phrase: "*Day by day, in every way, I am getting better and better.*" Do not think of anything particular, as the words "*in every way*" apply to everything.

Make this autosuggestion with confidence, with faith, with the certainty of obtaining what you want. The greater the conviction, the greater and the more rapid will be the results obtained.

Further, every time in the course of the day or night that you feel any distress physical or mental, immediately *affirm to yourself* that you will not consciously contribute to it, and that you are going to make it disappear; then passing your hand over your forehead, if it is something mental, or over the part which is painful, if it is something physical, repeat *extremely quickly*, moving your lips, the words: "It is going, it is going---", etc., etc., as long as may be necessary. With a little practice the physical or mental distress will have vanished in 20 to 25 seconds. Begin again whenever it is necessary. Avoid carefully any effort in practicing autosuggestion. (Inside Front Cover)

## ADDITIONAL EXCERPTS:

Autosuggestion—The implanting of an idea in oneself by oneself.

When the will and the imagination are antagonistic, it is always the imagination which wins, *without any exception.*

*It is impossible to think of two things at once*, that is to say that two ideas may be in juxtaposition, but they cannot be superimposed in our mind.

*Every thought entirely filling our mind becomes true for us and tends to transform itself into action.*
What conclusion is to be drawn from all this?

The conclusion is very simple and can be expressed in a few words: We possess within us a force of incalculable power, which, when we handle it unconsciously is often prejudicial to us. If on the contrary we direct it in a conscious and wise manner, it gives us the mastery of ourselves and allows us not only to escape and to aid others to escape, from physical and mental ills, but also to live in relative happiness, whatever the conditions in which we may find ourselves.

Lastly, and above all, it should be applied to the moral regeneration of those who have wandered from the right path.

Source: *Self Mastery Through Conscious Autosuggestion.* American Library Service. 1922. Inside Front Cover and additional excerpts.

---

## InHABITing Pattern #2: A Practice
*Self-Confidence Formula*
by Napoleon Hill

1. I know that I have the ability to achieve the object of my definite purpose in life; therefore,

I *demand* of myself persistent, continuous action toward its attainment, and I here and now promise to render such action.

2. I realize the dominating thoughts of my mind will eventually reproduce themselves in outward, physical action, and gradually transform themselves into physical reality; therefore, I will concentrate my thought, for thirty minutes daily, upon the task of thinking of the person I intend to become, thereby creating in my mind a clear mental picture.

3. I know through the principle of autosuggestion, any desire that I persistently hold in my mind will eventually seek expression through some practical means of attaining the object back of it; therefore, I will devote ten minutes daily to demanding of myself the development of *self-confidence*.

4. I have clearly written down a description of my *definite chief aim* in life, and I will never stop trying, until I shall have developed sufficient self-confidence for its attainment.

5. I fully realize that no wealth or position can long endure, unless built upon truth and justice; therefore, I will engage in no transaction that does not benefit all whom it affects. I will succeed by attracting to myself the forces I wish to use, and the cooperation of other people. I will induce

others to serve me, because of my willingness to serve others. I will eliminate hatred, envy, jealousy, selfishness, and cynicism, by developing love for all humanity, because I know that a negative attitude toward others can never bring me success. I will cause others to believe in me, because I will believe in them, and in myself. I will sign my name to this formula, commit it to memory, and repeat it aloud once a day, with full faith that it will gradually influence my thoughts and actions so that I will become a self-reliant, and successful, person.

Back of this formula is a law of nature that no man has yet been able to explain. The name by which one calls this law is of little importance. The important fact about it is—it *works* for the glory and success of mankind, *if* it is used constructively. On the other hand, if used destructively, it will destroy just as readily. In this statement may be found a very significant truth, namely, that those who go down in defeat, and end their lives in poverty, misery, and distress, do so because of negative application of the principle of autosuggestion. The cause may be found in the fact that all impulses of thought have a tendency to clothe themselves in their physical equivalent.

Source: *Think and Grow Rich*. Napoleon Hill. The Napoleon Hill Foundation. Collector's Edition. Pgs. 86 & 87.

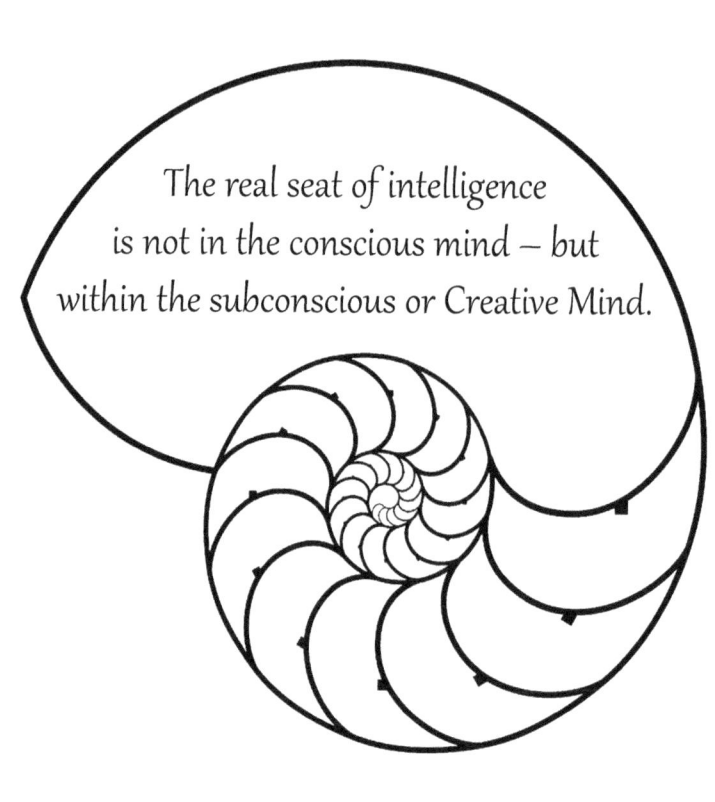

# TEXT No. 2

# YOU ARE A MIND WITH A BODY

BEFORE approaching this text, I'm going to suggest that you lay it aside for just a moment and mentally review your first one. Do you recall all of the seven steps? If not, delay reading this one for a few moments while you refreshen your memory. I want you to hold in mind the step regarding determination. If you will attack this text with a determination to make it mean a lot to you, it will.

We started the previous text by understanding that to get results in the least possible time, we would take up the application of principles before we had an explanation of them. Right now I will make a suggestion, and it will be some time before you are given an explanation; but if you will do what I say, you will gain results even before you understand **what is making the wheels go 'round.**

Would it sound strange if I should tell you that you are not a body with a mind? This, of course, is true. Instead, you are a mind with a body. From many people, this statement would call for a "so what?" But, after the full significance of this truth becomes apparent, you will have learned a very important fact.

That body of yours is just a utility for the mind. Think about it a moment and you'll begin to understand what I mean. To think of yourself as being a body with a mind, would be exactly like thinking of a house owning a man,—or a car owning the driver.

Now then, what can be gained by knowing this truth? What difference does it make whether we are a mind with a body, or a body with a mind? It makes all the difference in the world. It would appear inconceivable to imagine your car at times becoming stubborn and turning left when you would wish to go right;—or would back up when you wished to go forward. You know that, since you have full control of the car, such a thing would be out of the question.

That body of yours is at your service and will follow all of your mental directions;—after you once realize that **you are a mind with a body.**

Whenever we use a personal pronoun; "I," "Mine," "Me" or "My"—we are not referring to the physical body. We are referring to the mental self;—or spiritual self, if you wish to think of it as such.

In referring to your foot as "my foot" you mean just that;—it is a possession of your mental self. When you walk, your feet carry you forward because it is your will that they do so. You can't even imagine a case where they would refuse to obey instructions,—at least so long as you are free from any injury or malady which effects personal locomotion.

Whenever you use the expression: "I can't do this," or "I can't stop that," you are admitting that you have no control over your physical being and that it dictates to you instead of accepting dictation.

Right now I want to establish an important fact;—**you are the master of your being.** So,—to properly impress this truth upon your mind, declare to yourself: **I am MASTER of my BEING.** Repeat it several times. Think about it. Know it to be true. Realize that every part of your body is at your service—to do as you command;—**because it is your body.**

## OUR TWO MINDS

You have learned that you are a mind with a body. This indicates that the mind is singular—one mind. Probably it is true that we have but one mind,—but since it functions in a dual capacity, it will be helpful to think of it as two minds,—normally referred to as the **conscious** and **subconscious** mind.

The conscious mind does all the conscious thinking, reasoning, planning. The subconscious or that which I prefer to think of as the **Creative Mind**—takes care of all the involuntary operations of the body; breathing, beating of the heart, circulation of the blood, restoration of worn tissue, digestion of food, etc. None of these operations are performed with any aid from the conscious mind. In fact, the conscious mind does not possess sufficient intelligence to care for any of these functions. And, this brings us to another important truth: **THE REAL SEAT OF INTELLIGENCE IS NOT IN THE CONSCIOUS MIND—BUT WITHIN THE SUBCONSCIOUS OR CREATIVE MIND!**

If we were to stop right here and say no more regarding the powers of the Creative Mind, we would have indicated that the intelligence of this great mind goes even beyond our conscious comprehension;—but this is just the beginning of what we will learn regarding the reservoir of power and intelligence contained within the subconscious or Creative Mind.

Have you ever had a problem facing you and you were not sure as to the best solution,—and you said you would "sleep on it over night?" Have you noticed on the following day, your reasoning regarding the problem would seem a bit more logical than it did the night before? Without realizing it, you have used one of the basic principles of putting the Creative Mind to work for you.

The Creative Mind has reasoning faculties independent of the conscious mind. While the conscious mind is devoted to thoughts along one line, the subconscious or Creative Mind can be reasoning along lines of an entirely different nature. And, it is doing this continually; sometimes working for you and often against you.

The Creative Mind does not originate new thoughts through the process of thinking,—but works on the thoughts current in the conscious mind. If the conscious mind is holding negative thoughts, the Creative Mind will respond with negative reactions. Fortunately, the reverse is true. If the conscious mind is maintaining positive thoughts,—you will definitely gain positive reactions.

Right at this point, lay this text down for a few moments and repeat to yourself—at least three times: **"I am Happy."** After you have done this, you will understand what I mean. Your Creative Mind will accept the thought and begin working on it, and soon you will discover a feeling of uplift over your entire body. You see, you are a mind with a body—and your body responds to the dictates of your conscious mind.

Now then, if your Creative Mind will react on the thought: **"I am Happy."** It will likewise respond to all other thoughts—whether good or bad, depending upon the thoughts you maintain.

You wouldn't intentionally throw a monkey wrench in the gears if you knew it would wreck the machinery, would you? Not likely. Well, now that you know that negative thoughts create negative reactions, you will know that each time you permit entrance to a negative thought, you are literally dropping a monkey wrench into your mental gears. Of course, you'll no longer do such a thing.

All right, with this little explanation of the two minds,—I will lay out a routine for you to follow during the coming week. Remember, you are **not to proceed** with these texts more rapidly than one each week. To do so will **reduce** the amount of good you might expect from the **Magic Formula**. It would be a splendid idea to set aside a certain time on a certain day each week when you will approach a new text.— After you have done so, do not permit anything short of an emergency to take the time from you. This, in itself, will prove good practice in self-discipline.

The results you will obtain from this course will be tremendous. At this point it will be hard for you to conceive of the good which can come into your life as a result of your knowing and using the Magic Formula. You have already had results from Text No. 1, and now if you will follow the steps to be given,— you will gain even greater results from this text.

**STEP 1.** Starting tonight, and continuing until tomorrow evening,—each time you think of it,—repeat to yourself: *"I happily accept my present conditions as they are to act as a foundation on which to build. I have no self-pity for any sacrifices I might have been making;*

nor am I envious of others who might have more than I have. I know that I possess the power and intelligence which will enable me to gain what I want in life and I am grateful for what I have at present, whether humble or otherwise."

**STEP 2.** The admonition to follow is to be repeated several times during the next twenty-four hours. *"My mind is free from worry because I am in direct contact with the source of power and intelligence which enables me to dissolve the cause of the worry. My Creative Mind will direct me in thought and action toward the elimination of my worries."*

In making these declarations, do not do so with a high-powered commanding spirit; instead, with an air of nonchalance as casual as you would say to yourself: "I guess I'll get a drink of water." And, with the same feeling of certainty of accomplishment as you would feel toward your ability to get the glass of water. By the end of the day it will amaze you to see the new attitude you'll take toward your worries. You will be eager to follow the many courses which will suggest themselves toward the solving of your problems.

**STEP 3.** The thoughts you are to hold during the third day are very important. Do not neglect them in the least. As often as you can, say to yourself—knowingly:—*"I am convinced beyond all doubt that through* *the Magic Formula I am achieving Self Mastery. Results obtained to date are unmistakable. A new and glorious life is unfolding before me."*

The most important time to make your affirmations is just before going to sleep at night. This gives your Creative Mind an opportunity to work all night in making a reality of your declarations. The Creative Mind never sleeps. It is on the job 24-hours each day and if not working for you, is usually working against you. If you drop off to sleep with negative thoughts the Creative Mind will work on them. If, on the other hand, you wisely implant positive thoughts in your Creative Mind, you will be rewarded with positive reactions.

**STEP 4.** Not every person belongs to the class of "scatter brains," but it is a fact that only a small percentage of people can concentrate for long on any single thought. Naturally the more you are able to concentrate, the greater will be the results from the Magic Formula. In this connection, the admonition designed for use during the fourth day will prove invaluable. Each time you think of it—repeat to yourself in a positive, yet matter-of-fact way: *"I am blessed with great powers of mental concentration. I can hold my thoughts on a single idea until I elect to discharge it from my mind."* It is important that while making these statements you do so with a definite feeling of confidence. In fact, do not even question the efficacy of the declarations. To do so means the setting up of a mental conflict which might have a neutralizing effect on the good which could result.

**STEP 5.** By the time you reach the fifth day on Text 2, you will not have too much need for the affirmation which follows,—yet, use it faithfully during the day and evening as the results will strengthen those already obtained. *"Each day I have a greater ambition to carry on with the new and constructive ideas which are flowing into consciousness."* In a later text, you will learn that we think in terms of pictures. Even before you reach that point, it will be helpful if you, while following through these steps, mentally picture the condition you are talking about. For example,— with this last step, can't you close your eyes and actually see yourself enthusiastically climbing toward greater success and happiness?

**STEP 6.** You'll enjoy this step, because through it, you will reach a point of mental peace more pleasant, perhaps, than you have ever experienced before. For a full day, each time you think of it, repeat to yourself with a great feeling of joy: *"I am at peace with myself and the world. Problems facing me are no longer disturbing because I have made contact with my true source of intelligence and power. I am guided to do the* *right thing at the right time."* Should anything happen of a disturbing nature,—calmly repeat this positive statement and notice how quickly you'll assume the role of master.

**STEP 7.** There will be no specific affirmation for this, the seventh day. Instead, without the use of the printed text, mentally review the various steps. Sense a feeling of joy as you look back over the accomplishments of the past two weeks, and know that your new life of greater abundance is merely getting off to a very good start.

Do not start Text 3 until the following day **after** your review. And a good practice, before starting any new text, is to meditate a few minutes in reflecting over the previous ones so that you will get yourself in the mood for your new lesson.

Under **no** circumstances start a new text while mentally upset or while under a strain of any kind. Be sure to approach the monograph only when comfortable and **fully relaxed;**—and without **anything** troubling the mind.

Continue making notes as you proceed. You have plenty of space for them, and later they will prove helpful when you review former texts. In addition to marginal notes,—it is also well to underscore any statements which particularly impress you.

Hasn't this text been stimulating? And let me conclude as usual.

*May Joy and Peace Be Yours!*

> Each day I have a greater ambition to carry on with the new and constructive ideas which are flowing into consciousness.
>
> I am at peace with myself and the world. Problems facing me are no longer disturbing because I have made contact with my true source of intelligence and power. I am guided to do the right thing at the right time.
>
> I am convinced through all doubt that through the Magic Formula I am achieving Self Mastery. Results obtained to date are unmistakable. A new and glorious life is unfolding before me.
>
> I am blessed with great powers of mental concentration. I can hold my thoughts on a single idea until I elect to discharge it from my mind.
>
> I happily accept my present conditions as they are to act as a foundation on which to build. I have no self-pity for any sacrifices I might have been making; nor am I envious of others who might have more than I have. I know that I possess the power and intelligence which will enable me to gain what I want in life and I am grateful for what I have at present, whether humble or otherwise.
>
> My mind is free from worry because I am in direct contact with the source of power and intelligence which enables me to dissolve the cause of the worry. My Creative Mind will direct me in thought and action toward the elimination of my worries.

## InHABITing Pattern #3: A Suggestion
### *Action for Success*
### by Dorothea Brande

Fortunately, it is not at all necessary to be put under the sway of another's will in order to do our own work. The solution is far simpler. All that is necessary to break the spell of inertia and frustration is this:

*Act as if it were impossible to fail.*

That is the talisman, the formula, the command of

right-about-face which turns us from failure towards success.

Source: *Wake Up and Live!* Dorothea Brande. Simon and Schuster. 1936. Pgs. 79-80.

## InHABITing Pattern #4: A Practice
### *The Mirror Technique*
### by Claude Bristol

Stand in front of a mirror. It need not be a full-length mirror, but it should be of sufficient size so that you may at least see your body from the waist up.

Those of you who have been in the army know what it means to come to attention—stand fully erect, bring your heels together, pull in your stomach, keep your chest out and your head up. Now breathe deeply three or four times until you feel a sense of power, strength, and determination. Next, look into the very depths of your eyes, tell yourself that you are going to get what you want—name it aloud so you can see your lips move and you can hear the words uttered. Make a regular ritual of it, practice doing it at least twice a day, mornings and evenings—and you will be surprised at the results. You can augment this by writing with soap on the face of the mirror any slogans or key words you wish, so long as they are the key to what you have previously visualized and want to see in reality. Within a few days you will have developed a sense of confidence that you never realized you could build within yourself.

As you stand before the mirror, keep telling yourself that you are going to be an outstanding success and that nothing in this world is going to stop you. Does this sound silly? Don't forget that every idea presented to the subconscious mind is going to be produced in its exact counterpart in objective life, and the quicker your subconscious gets the idea, the sooner your wish becomes a picture of power. Certainly it is not good business for you to tell anyone of the devices you employ, because you might be ridiculed by scoffers and your confidence shaken, especially if you are just beginning to learn the science.

Source: *The Magic of Believing*. Claude Bristol. Prentice-Hall, Inc. 1948. Pgs. 146-147.

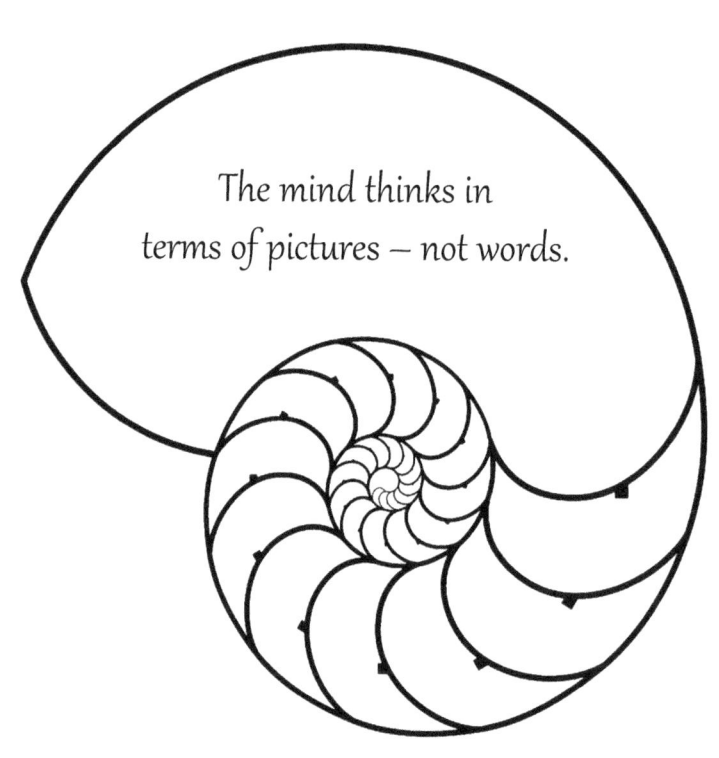

## TEXT No. 3

# PICTURES ARE PATTERNS

YOU are not to start this text for at least five minutes;—and this is what you are to do in the meantime. Make yourself comfortable,—and get yourself in an *extremely* happy frame of mind. Review the good which has come to you already,—and know that it is just starting. So, put a song in your heart—get a glad-to-be-alive feeling, then you're ready to go.

Make this a ritual from now on. Never take up any text until you get yourself in a favorable frame of mind. **Be Happy!** Those are your watch words. If text time arrives and you cannot get yourself in the right mood—**WAIT**. However, the very thought of these texts will bring a glow of happiness to you because you will look at them as great liberators,—freeing you from failure, gloom and poor health.

All right,—are the five minutes up? And are you Happy? Extremely Happy? Let's start!

In this lesson I'm going to put you on a diet. Oh, don't be frightened;—it will have nothing at all to do with the food you eat.—This will be a mental diet.

You learned in the first text that negative thoughts produce negative reactions—and positive thoughts produce positive reactions.

On the instrument board of your automobile are several instruments keeping you informed as to the amount of gasoline in the tank; temperature of your motor; condition of the battery, etc. If the gasoline gauge indicates your fuel is getting low, you look for the first service station so that you may fill your tank. If the motor seems too hot,—you investigate the condition of your radiator and look after the water supply. You would not think of driving nonchalantly while the instruments were pointing to danger.

I often wish nature had provided a meter whereby we could see thought—or at least one which would register the type of thought, whether negative or **positive**. If there were a needle which would dip into the **red** when thoughts were **negative**—and swing over into a **green**, let us say, when thoughts were **positive**, we would change our thoughts immediately when we could see the needle lean toward the **negative** side.

In eliminating negative thoughts, it might be well to think a bit about the causes of negative thoughts, because, after all, they are not causes themselves, but **effects** from **causes**.

**Worry** and **fear** both cause negative thoughts. Naturally, it is easy to tell you to stop worrying and overcome your fear,—but, you might tell me it is not quite as easy for you to accomplish, such a feat. All right,—why do you worry? Worry is nothing more nor less than evidence of lack of faith in yourself. You fear things are going to happen and you are afraid you are not big enough to cope with the situation when it arrives,—isn't that so? No, you do not think of worry in this light,— but think about it;—you'll find this to be true. Now then,—although you have just started learning something about creative psychology, you have gained sufficient results to already convince yourself that, through the vast amount of intelligence and power you have at your command—through your **Creative Mind**—you will prove equal to any occasion. So, think of your worries as problems and know that there is a solution to every problem—otherwise it would not be a problem. I am sure you will now be able to smile at your so called worries and know—with a feeling of pride—that you are much bigger than they are, and they will soon be dissolved. So, we can eliminate this cause of negative thoughts.

**Sense** of **inadequacy** will cause negative thoughts— many of them. With this type of a personality, one will feel his efforts are not productive; he will not have confidence in his ability to accomplish anything worthwhile. He therefore fears losing his job or business. This type of individual fears everything. He doubts his ability to win or hold the love of those who could mean so much to him. Naturally, with such a complex it is easy to see how his mental meter (Let's call it a Thought-o-meter) would usually show the needle dipped into the **red** or negative side. If this should be true with you, **how** will you take care of it? You can answer this question as well as I can. You **know** that you are a mind with a body and that you can truthfully say: **I am master!** You know you are improving in **everything** which gives you every reason to keep the needle on the **positive** side.

**Fear** of **death** definitely will cause the old needle to camp on the negative side. If you fear death, you become afraid of every pain or ache, feeling that they might be danger signals. You will have a horror of birthdays, knowing each-one brings you a step closer to your departure. Very well, what will we do about such thoughts? Here is something which will appeal to your logical mind. A happy mind is conducive to better health, and with better health you will naturally live longer; won't you? Right? Well, the thing to do is to **love life** but **do not fear death**. And as you progress with this Magic Formula you will have reasons galore for being happy. So, we'll keep the needle out of the **red**, so far as this fear is concerned, won't we?

**Jealousy** does not show up well on your thought-o-meter, does it? Jealousy over things and people is very negative. And, why do some people show jealousy? Viewing this question through the eyes of a psychologist, it is obvious that jealousy is caused by one or both of two reasons: **inferiority** or **selfishness**. Should you by

## TEXT NO. 3 - PICTURES ARE PATTERNS

any remote possibility be effected by the former,—I am certain the Magic Formula is changing the picture—completely. And, if selfishness should be causing jealousy, you'll lose that too,—because once you become accustomed to tapping the **reservoir** of **power** contained in your Creative Mind, you'll find no reason for being selfish. You'll radiate so much charm and magnetism, your loved ones will be drawn closer to you.

**Hatred** is negative;—so much so, it greatly impairs one's health. Hatred harms no one except the one holding the hatred. Here is a suggestion which some might not understand. If you think you have reason for hating anyone, do not do it, **bless** him instead. The very doing so brings a glow of happiness to your heart—and happiness puts you on the **positive** side and brings with it great rewards. From now on you will hold no hatred for **anyone,** will you?

A **bad disposition** is negative. And a bad disposition is not a cause, it's an effect. What is causing it? Correct the cause and you will no longer have a bad disposition. A few of the causes of a bad disposition are: -
   a. A guilty consciousness will cause a bad disposition. If we have done something we should **not** have done, we find ourselves constantly on edge, fearing it might be discovered. Naturally, under such circumstances, one's disposition is not too angelic.
   b. Unfinished tasks do not help one's disposition. Starting the day facing a quantity of unfinished

jobs will usually cause irritability. They detract from that glad-to-be-alive feeling. It is very good practice to clean-up as we proceed. It is a wonderful feeling each time a job is completed.
c. Disliking the things you are doing will cause a bad disposition. Learn to like what you are doing, or find things to do which you like, if that is at all possible.
d. Poor health often effects the disposition,—but, of course, you'll watch your health.

The moment you take steps to correct a bad disposition, you will find the **Thought-O-Meter needle literally** jumping to the **positive** side.

## MENTAL PICTURES

The mind thinks in terms of pictures—not words. Everything we see and hear we translate into mental pictures;—in other words we see the thoughts. If I should mention Automobile you do not see the letters comprising the word a-u-t-o-m-o-b-i-l-e. You see a picture of a car. It might be your own—one you are familiar with or would like to own. In any event, you see an automobile. When it is not possible to picture a thought, your mind does the next best thing and symbolizes. If the word "Love" is mentioned, you cannot see love, but you are quite likely to see a mental picture of one you love. The same is true with such words as joy, happiness, friend, hatred, etc.

Imagination is one's ability to mentally picture things and conditions which do not exist. There is **constructive** imagination which sees everything through **positive** eyes, and there is, I am sorry to say, **negative** imagination which is just the opposite.

In a later text we will learn that the pictures we hold in our conscious mind act as **patterns** for the Creative mind which acts upon them, **reproducing** them in our bodies and affairs.

But, we will not wait for that text before we gain good from mental pictures. We'll start **right now**. And, this brings us back to the very first statement made in this text. You were told that you would be put on a diet:—a mental diet. And that is what I propose to do now.

When you eat the wrong food, you frequently suffer from indigestion. If you allow your mind to be filled with wrong thoughts—wrong mental pictures— you'll suffer from mental indigestion.

Picture magazines such as *Life, Look, Pix,* etc. employ the services of capable editors, whose job it is to select from the thousand pictures submitted, those which will enhance the value of the publications and attract more subscribers. Carelessness in selecting pictures could greatly depreciate the value of the picture magazine.

You are to act as picture editor from now in editing

the mental pictures which you permit to enter your mind. Worry is nothing more than the holding of mental pictures of things we do **not want**. True? Fear is the same. In fact, all of the negative thoughts we have mentioned, plus numerous more you can think of,—pictures of the wrong kind. They will wreck your happiness, effect your health, hold you back from making the progress in life you might otherwise have a right to expect.

There is no such thing as a vacuum in Nature. You can't take away something without replacing it with something else. So, knowing this, if a mental picture of a negative nature creeps into your mind,—remove it by putting a positive **picture** in its place.

Your work for this week is very simple,—yet important—**vitally** important. Make it **positive thought week**. Watch your thoughts and eliminate negative ones. Guard against negative conversation—because it surely creates negative mental pictures.

To make certain **positive thought week** will be effective,—suppose we plant a positive-thought seed in our Creative Mind—right now! Read the following statement at least three times, s-l-o-w-l-y and thoughtfully. *Each time a negative thought attempts to enter my mind, I will immediately become aware of it and will dissolve it with a positive thought. My self confidence is mounting as day by day I gain greater mastery over self.*

I might suggest at this point that you refrain from looking for results the moment you first make a declaration. Just calmly make the statement with assurance that results will be forthcoming. If you plant a seed you do not see anything the first moment after planting, but you know that, if you care for and nourish the seed, in due time you will be rewarded with a plant and blossoms. Perhaps a good attitude to take is the one you assume when you drop a letter into the mail box. You do not expect to find an answer upon your return to your home. No,—you simply drop the letter into the slot and know without specific thinking—that through a chain of events—in due time a reply will reach you. Be just as casual when you make an affirmation. It is just as well not to think about it immediately after making the statement, because when you do, a bit of doubt or skepticism might creep in, thereby nullifying any effect which might otherwise be manifest.

At this point I could enter into a long discussion regarding the principles soon to be put to use. In fact, in my former works on Creative Psychology, in the very early lessons I would devote much space to an explanation of why the principles would work for you. In this course we are reversing our procedure and are first learning how to apply the principles and then later we will learn why. In this way we are gaining benefits right from the start. You have already profited, immeasurably, from the first texts, I am sure,—and we'll keep the result mounting throughout the entire course.

*May Joy and Peace Be Yours!*

## InHABITing Pattern #5: A Practice
*Desire*
by Claude Bristol

It was desire that brought progress to the world. Without it, we all would still be living in a primitive age. Everything we have in our modern world is the result of desire. Indeed, desire is the motivating force of life itself. You see it all around you—in the animal kingdom, in all forms of plant life, and in all acts and operations of human beings. Hunger promotes a desire for food, poverty a desire for riches, cold causes us to desire warmth, inconveniences a desire for better things.

It's the generating power of all human action, and without it no one can get very far. The keener, the more urgent the desire, the sooner its consummation. It marks the difference between the uneducated ditchdigger and the person of accomplishment, between the clerk and the executive, between the failure and the success. So you must start with desire, keeping in mind that with the magic of believing you can obtain what you picture in your mind's eye. The mechanics are for the purpose of helping you to focus sharply your desire-picture on the screen of your subconscious mind, as well as enable you to shut off and keep out all distracting thoughts, negative ideas, or any fear or doubt projections that might otherwise penetrate to your subconscious.

So, let's get down to the mechanics. Secure three or

four cards. Ordinary business-size cards will do. In your office, your home, your room, or any other place where you can have privacy, sit down and ask yourself what you desire above everything else. When the answer comes and you are certain that it is your uppermost desire, then at the top of one card write a word picture of it. One or two words may be sufficient—a job, a better job, more money, a home of your own. Then on each card duplicate the word picture on the original. Carry one in your billfold, or handbag, place another alongside your bed or fasten it to your bedstead, place another on your shaving mirror or dressing table, and still another on your desk. The whole idea, as you may have guessed, it to enable you to see mentally the picture at all hours of the day. Just before going to sleep at night and upon waking in the mornings are highly important moments of the twenty-four hours in which to concentrate upon your thoughts with added force. But don't stop with merely those two periods, for the more often you can visualize the desire by this method (or by one of your own devising), the speedier the materialization.

At the start you may have no idea of how the results are to come. Yet you need not concern yourself. Just leave it to the subconscious mind, which has its own ways of making contacts, and of opening doors and avenues that you may never have even thought of. You will receive assistance from the most unexpected sources. You will find that ideas useful in the accomplishment of your program will come at the most unexpected times. You may be suddenly struck with the idea of seeing a person you have not heard from for a long time, or calling upon a man you have never seen before. You may get the idea of writing a letter or making a telephone call. Whatever the idea is, follow it. Keep a pad and pencil on a stand near the head of your bed, and when these ideas come during the night, note them on a pad, so they will not be forgotten by morning. Many successful people get ideas during the night that are immediately transcribed to a pad so they will not be lost.

Source: *The Magic of Believing*. Claude Bristol. Prentice-Hall, Inc. 1948. Pgs. 118-119.

## InHABITing Pattern #6: A Practice
*Six Ways to turn Desires into Gold*
by Napoleon Hill

The method by which DESIRE for riches can be transmuted into its financial equivalent, consists of six definite, practical steps, viz:

**First.** Fix in your mind the *exact* amount of money you desire. It is not sufficient merely to say "I want plenty of money." Be definite as to the amount. (There is a psychological reason for definiteness which will be described in a subsequent chapter.)

**Second.** Determine exactly what you intend to give in return for the money you desire. (There is no such reality as "something for nothing.")

**Third.** Establish a definite date when you intend to *possess* the money you desire.

**Fourth.** Create a definite plan for carrying out your desire, and begin *at once,* whether you are ready or not, to put this plan into *action.*

**Fifth.** Write out a clear, concise statement of the amount of money you intend to acquire, name the time limit for its acquisition, state what you intend to give in return for the money, and describe clearly the plan through which you intend to accumulate it.

**Sixth.** Read your written statement aloud, twice daily, once just before retiring at night, and once after arising in the morning. AS YOU READ—SEE AND FEEL AND BELIEVE YOURSELF ALREADY IN POSSESSION OF THE MONEY.

It is important that you follow the instructions described in these six steps. It is especially important that you observe, and follow the instructions in the sixth paragraph. You may complain that it is impossible for you to "see yourself in possession of money" before you actually have it. Here is where a BURNING DESIRE will come to your aid. If you truly DESIRE money so keenly that your desire is an obsession, you will have no difficulty in convincing yourself that you will acquire it. The object is to want money, and to become so determined to have it that you CONVINCE yourself you will have it.

Source. *Think and Grow Rich.* Napoleon Hill. The Ralston Society. 1937. Pgs. 42-43.

# TEXT No. 4

# THE MAGIC FORMULA

**ARE** you comfortable? Are you relaxed? Are you **happy?** If your answer to these three questions is in the affirmative, then you can proceed with this text.

If you were presented with an Aladdin's Lamp, it couldn't mean as much to you as this particular text will mean.

Each of us, at some time in our lives, have wished that we could have some means to raise us above the level of struggle, and to be able to enjoy the good things in life. If the road ahead looks steep—and the burdens we are bearing seem to be weighting us down—an easy way out would look mighty good to us. Under such conditions we often resort to day dreaming. We picture ourselves being left a fortune, and we try to imagine how wonderful it would feel to be able to laugh at financial and other worries.

During our hours of dream-wishing, Aladdin's Lamp often appeals to us as the answer. We do not wish a relative would pass on just to satisfy our desire for wealth,—so we permit our imagination to drift, often as in Childhood, to the fairy tale type of inheritance.

Should such wishes come true,—while they might relieve your mind of financial worries, they would not—**could not**—make you happy. True happiness comes through achievement. Do you think the beggar enjoys the meal which has been given to him as much as the man who pays for his meal with coin he has earned?

You can have the good things in life. You can have riches. You can have an abundance of the worldly goods which, perhaps, up to now you have merely envied. And, yes, you can have them on a basis of tremendous satisfaction, because they will come to you through your own efforts. As you proudly make use of your valued possessions, you can do so with a feeling of pride, because it was through your own creative ability you acquired them.

Right now I will begin putting you to work on principles which I would have hesitated giving to you sooner. You would have had difficulty in accepting them, because the promise they hold is so great. But knowing what you have achieved up to now—assuming, of course, you have carefully followed all suggestions given—I know you will continue to follow instructions knowing that nothing but tested and proved principle will be given to you.

In an earlier text you were told that your Creative Mind is the storehouse of intelligence and power. Up to now you have not been told how to contact that power. Yes, you are using it, but, without knowing too much as to what goes on behind the veil of consciousness.

Perhaps one of the questions which has come to your mind is: "How do I contact this source of power and intelligence?" The answer is simple;—so simple in fact, that, if you had not already felt the results from such contact,—you would find it hard to accept that which will now be given. The personal pronoun "I" is the switch which makes the contact. You have already learned that you are a **mind with a body**. Referring to yourself as "I" does not mean that you are referring to your body at all;—you are referring to your mind. And, when using this personal pronoun, you are going down much deeper than merely your conscious mind. You are addressing your entire mental self which includes your conscious and Creative Mind.

The only difference between people who do things and those who do not, is a matter of consciousness. One thinks in terms of "I Can" the other "I Can't." That's all. When you knowingly say "I can do this" **you can,** because you are putting your forces to work to create the condition necessary to bring the objective into being. Your Creative Mind not only supplies you with the enthusiasm to work on your project, but supplies your conscious mind with guidance as to the various steps to take. An air of confidence is developed which attracts the confidence and cooperation of others. The road of possibilities and opportunities appear to open up before you.

When you say: "I can't do this" you literally close your mental door so far as creative effort is concerned. But, the unfortunate part is, your Creative Mind accepts the negative as an instruction and proceeds to build upon that by making you gloomy instead of enthusiastic;—and instead of causing your personality to be magnetic, it actually makes it just the opposite.

Today you begin mapping your life just as you want it. From now on you will not live a hit or miss—trial and error—existence. You will live a planned life—and it will be one of your own making. You will know what next year and the years to follow will bring because you have planned them.

With only one exception we will plan our lives in units of five years. It is hard to conceive exactly what you would like to do and to have, let us say, ten years from now. You can, however, be quite certain of the many things you would like to have brought into being during a period of five years. So, let us think in term of five-year periods;—except so far as the matter of health and general well being is concerned. We want to know we will have good health and an alert and active mind for a great many years. And, in a text soon

## TEXT NO. 4 - THE MAGIC FORMULA

to come, we will learn how easy it is to really feel fine.

Can you imagine how a small boy would feel if he were told to put on trousers with large pockets because he was to be taken into a wondrous cave of candy, marbles, games and just about everything which would warm the heart of a boy, and that he could fill his pockets with anything he wished? Well, now I am going to make a promise to you which will be just about as thrilling. I will start you on the road toward getting almost anything you want in life.

Obtain a blank book to be used as your plan book. You may obtain one at the stationery counter in any 10¢ store. Before writing anything down, meditate for a while and ask yourself this question: "If I could have anything I wanted, what do I want?" Think about it very seriously. Forget your limitations for the moment. Just picture yourself in a situation where you can help yourself to anything: money, house, car, better job,—a business of your own. What would you take under such conditions?

As your **wants** crystallize in your mind, write them down. Take a page for possessions and a page for your affairs. On the former, list everything you would like to own of a material nature, and do not be afraid to be generous with yourself. Do not put down **dimes** if you want **dollars**. On the second sheet put down those things which pertain to your affairs; your job, business, friendships, etc. Think in terms of five years. List those changes which you would like to have take place during this period. Before the end of this five-year period you will want to repeat this procedure and plan for the next five years.

Now here comes a vitally important instruction. At least twice each day, refer to this book and before reading the items listed, repeat this statement to yourself: "I am guided to take the steps necessary to bring my listed objectives into being." Then slowly read each item you have on both lists.

Do you recall what you learned regarding mental pictures? All right,—as you see each item on the pages of your book,—go beyond merely seeing the word—see, in your mind's eye, that which you desire—and see yourself in connection with it. If an objective is a fine new home, really see yourself living in such a home. If an objective is a better job—or a business of your own, see **yourself** actively engaged in the better job—or business. Under no circumstances look at the list with the feeling that you are wishing for those things mentioned. Read the items and as you do so, sense a feeling of joy that you are mentally viewing those things which are coming to you.

If you were to receive a letter from an attorney in which he listed many valuable properties which were willed to you,—every time you reviewed the letter you would have a feeling of great happiness in anticipation of things soon to be yours. You would not read the letter and wish for those things, because you were **convinced** they were about to be yours. Well, this is just the feeling I want you to have as you look over your lists of objectives.

If you have been following the texts very carefully up to now, you have gained a success consciousness which knows **no** defeat and it will not be difficult for you to fully accept the thoughts given in this one. You will be exuberant as you realize that you have possession of the key which will enable you to get what you really want from life.

In Text Number 3 worry was discussed a bit and now this subject can be brought up again for further consideration. The mind, as you know, thinks in terms of pictures—not words. Worry is nothing more nor less than holding **mental pictures of things you do not want.**

What you have learned in this text will help materially to overcome worry because you will be training yourself to think in terms of things you want, instead of otherwise.

At this point I would like to inject a bit of warning. Students will often feel it is not necessary to write the objectives down,—that will be simple to keep them in mind and refer to them mentally instead of referring to the written list continually. It would be decided unwise to do this. Seeing the objectives in written form helps to impress them on your mind much stronger than though you make the operation fully a mental one.

You may vary this procedure, however, Some students, instead of using a plain blank book for their objectives will obtain a large scrap book and assign a full page to each objective and in addition to writing down the name of the objective, will secure pictures and paste them in the objective page. This is good, of course, and makes it even easier to visualize.

It is advisable to cross off your objectives as they come into being. Seeing them checked off from day to day heightens your enthusiasm toward the others which are in the process of materialization. This is easy to understand.

You will find at times you will decide you do not want certain objectives which you have listed. In such a case, cross them out. On the other hand you will continually think of new objectives which have not been listed. These should be added. In other words, keep your objective lists up-to-date.

You might ask if you may add objectives which are not directly for you, but which are for some one near and dear to you. This is all right. In fact, if it makes you happy to be of service to others, then, any objective you hold in mind for them is, in reality, for you.

Let me make it clear that the thoughts given in this text are not in any way related to magic. It is not my contention that by listing objectives and then reviewing them daily will invoke any spirits which will make these objectives appear as if by magic. What really happens is that the procedure is enabling you to build a success consciousness and with a success consciousness, your Creative Mind, with its reasoning power, will guide you toward doing the things which will bring the objectives into being.

You would not want it any other way. As stated in a previous text, the real satisfaction of success is in the achieving. Our greatest thrill comes as we see the fruits of our efforts coming into being.

A final thought regarding your objectives relates to the happiness they may give you. Students will frequently ask how they can know if they will be happy after they get their objectives. The answer to this question is quite simple. If the objective is wanted through selfish reasons,—you'll be able to get it—but it is doubtful if you'll be happy very long after you do get it. If your desire for an objective is unselfish, you need have no fear. You will be happy when you acquire it.

As Text 4 comes to an end, suppose, without referring to the former texts, you try to review them beginning with the first one. And, in your review, make an inventory of the results you have obtained to date. It would be a good idea to take a sheet of paper and write down the number of each text and after it, briefly mention the main point gained from that particular monograph and results obtained. If you do that for each one of the three previous texts, you will be surprised to find how much good you are obtaining from your Magic Formula.

Remember, what you will get out of your study will be in direct proportion to what you put into it. If you take every text seriously and follow the simple suggestions given, you will not be able to appraise in terms of money the value this course will be to you.

And now;—*May Joy and Peace Be Yours!*

## InHABITing Pattern #7: A Meditation
*I Need Be No Failure!*
By Maltbie D. Babcock, D.D.

Here we have reached the splendid truth—I need be no failure! Come what may, succeed or fail what will, I need be no failure. My field may be stony or swampy, my plough may be poor, my strength small, the weather bad; but if heartily as unto my Lord I do the best I can and look not back but keep right on, I am no failure.

To have a fair wind and a sunny sky and a tight boat is not necessarily to be a success, and to have head-winds and cross-cut tides and rain and cold and hunger is not of necessity to be a failure; but no matter what the weather does, no matter what the tides,—rain or shine, snow or blow, to steer by the stars and with a true heart to keep the course as best I can, is to succeed and be no failure, though my boat goes down and I am no more known till the sea gives up its dead.

Failure, then, is never an absolute word—always relative; and the only real failure is inside, not outside. It is not being true to the best we know. Inside failure is the only calamity. Outside failure may be the greatest blessing. Let me be loyal to plain and providential duty, true to the best I know, and what seems failure will prove to be a means of knowledge, development, and not seldom the bud of success.

Source: *The Success of Defeat*. Maltbie D. Babcock. D.D. Charles Scribner's Sons. 1905. Pgs. 5-7.

## InHABITing Pattern #8: A Reading
*Self-Suggestion, the Connecting Link Between the Conscious and the Subconscious Mind*
by Napoleon Hill

Transfer of thought from the conscious to the subconscious section of the mind may be hastened by the simple process of "stepping up" or stimulating the vibrations of thought through faith, fear, or any other highly intensified emotion, such as enthusiasm, a burning desire based on definiteness of purpose.

Thoughts backed by faith have precedence over all others in the matter of definiteness and speed with which they are handed over to the subconscious section of the mind and are acted upon. The speed with which the power of faith works has given rise to the belief held by many that certain phenomena are the result of "miracles."

Psychologists and scientists recognize no such phenomenon as a miracle, claiming as they do that everything which happens is the result of a definite cause, albeit a cause which cannot be explained. Be that as it may, it is a known fact that the person who is capable of freeing his mind from all self-imposed limitations, through the mental attitude known as faith, generally finds the solution to all of his problems, regardless of their nature.

Psychologists recognize also that Infinite Intelligence, while it is not claimed to be an automatic solver of riddles, nevertheless carries out to a logical conclusion any clearly defined idea, aim, purpose or desire that is submitted to the subconscious section of the mind in a mental attitude of perfect faith.

However, Infinite Intelligence never attempts to modify, change or otherwise alter any thought that is submitted to it, and it has never been known to act upon a mere wish or indefinite idea, thought or purpose. Get this truth well grounded in your mind and you will find yourself in possession of sufficient power to solve your daily problems with much less effort than most people devote to worrying over their problems.

So-called "hunches" often are signals indicating that Infinite Intelligence is endeavoring to reach and influence the conscious section of the mind, but you will observe that they usually come in response to some idea, plan, purpose or desire, or some fear that has been handed over to the subconscious section of the mind.

All "hunches" should be treated civilly and examined carefully, as they often convey, either in whole or in part, information of the utmost value to the individual who receives them. These "hunches" often make their appearance many hours, days or weeks after the thought which inspires them has reached the reservoir of Infinite Intelligence. Meanwhile, the individual often has forgotten the original thought which inspired them.

This is a deep, profound subject about which even the wisest of men know very little. It becomes a self-revealing subject only upon meditation and thought.

Understand the principle of mind operation here described and you will have a dependable clue as to why meditation sometimes brings that which one desires, while at other times it brings that which one does not wish.

Source: *The Master-Key to Riches*. Napoleon Hill. Willing Publishing Company. 1945. Pgs. 61-63.

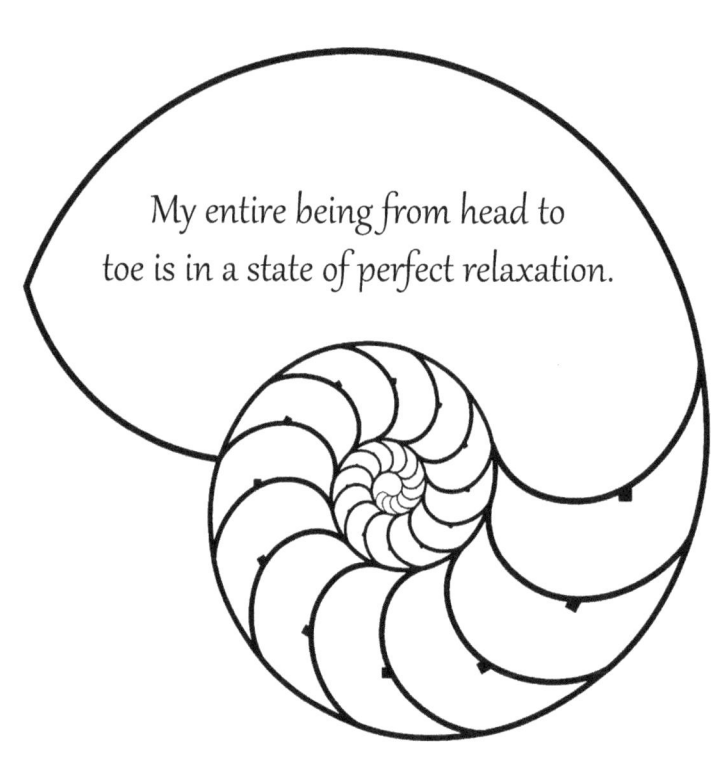

# TEXT No. 5

# PHYSICAL WELLNESS AND TENSENESS

*The Art of RELAXATION.*
*This Text shows you how to add to your energy and detract from fatigue.*


"I just can't relax." Three out of every four people will make this exact statement, and, perhaps, this might include you.

This text will be devoted to the art of relaxation,—and from what you know about the mind and the way it operates, you will never again make a statement such as that first given.

You **can** relax, because you're a **mind with a body** and that body will do what you direct it to do. Right now, before going a bit further,—try this experiment: Raise your right arm! Open and close your hand a few times. Wiggle your fingers! All right, that's enough of that. Did you have any difficulty in performing any one of those operations? Not a bit. Do you know why? Simply because you **knew you could do so.** You know without hesitation that your arms and legs and fingers and toes will do as you bid them to do. You have no doubt about it.

The muscles of the body will likewise respond to your mental instruction, so long as you know they will do so. Now then, since we are working on a result-first; theory-later basis,—right this minute we will give the Creative Mind its instructions regarding relaxation. Read the following statement at least three times, s-l-o-w-l-y and thoughtfully,—then set this text aside for a moment and allow your being to respond to your Creative Mind and relax—fully.

*"My entire being from head to toe is in a state of perfect relaxation. Tension has been released removing all physical restrictions, permitting blood to circulate freely through every vein, artery and capillary in my body. I sense a feeling of wholesome well-being as my body accumulates renewed energy."*

If you really meant what you said while repeating this affirmation,—right now you should not be conscious of any body at all. Complete relaxation means just that. You reach a state where you are almost a mind afloat. Being conscious of various members of the body indicates that you have not fully relaxed.

Here is a fact you should remember. When the body is tense, it is **burning energy;**—when relaxed, it is **storing energy.**

There are times when it is proper for the body to be tense. When performing difficult bits of work, you will become tense. When tense, you are using energy which is right under proper circumstances. That is why nature provides you energy. But, there are many, many moments during the day when you can relax, thus recapturing some, if not all, of the energy expended.

Unless one's work is extremely strenuous, there is no reason why he should be dead tired at the end of the day. He should reach his home to enjoy a good dinner and be able to thoroughly enjoy a pleasant evening. It is when one keeps himself tense all day long that he ends such a day utterly exhausted.

Some people wonder why they become so tired especially since they are sitting down so much. Sitting down is no indication that you are relaxed. You can be just as tense while seated as you can be while standing. As far as that goes, you can be tense while you are in bed. If you are one who awakes in the morning feeling about as tired as when you went to bed,—you have probably been tense all night, even though you may have slept. You have been burning energy while you should have been storing it. When you learn to go to bed and relax—you'll wake up in the morning anxious to start the day.

Did you ever know that you must relax mentally before you can relax physically? Yes, this is true. That body of yours reflects the state of your mind. If your mind is tense, your body will be likewise. Let me give you an example. Suppose that you are standing on the top of a very tall building. You are right on the edge of the roof looking down toward the street. You become very much interested in the midget people and automobiles you see a great distance below. As you imagine such a situation, picture yourself loosing your balance and falling to earth. In doing this, don't you feel your body growing tense?

Think of yourself alone in a canoe away from shore in very deep water. A storm comes-up and your boat capsizes. Don't you shudder as you hold such a mental picture? Or, I could give you the illustration of a small boy sucking on a large juicy lemon. What happens? Your mouth begins to water. All of these illustrations prove that we get physiological reactions from our thoughts. And, this being true,—you can understand how impossible it would be to become physically relaxed while the mind is tense. Usually, while making the affirmative statement previously given, your mind automatically relaxes, because you are thinking of relaxation. But, if the mind remains tense, if there is some problem on your mind—realize, that holding yourself tense will actually hold you back from finding a solution; in fact, matters are likely to become worse—but, if you master relaxation, you gain so much energy it becomes increasingly easy to handle your problems. So, if necessary, give your mind an instruction, such as: *"I am master! My mind is dwelling on peaceful, harmonious thoughts."*

You will be astounded to find how easy it will be for you to relax, both, mentally and physically, And, you will likewise be amazed to discover how much more energy you have. You will be able to do more and better work, with less fatigue than formerly. You will do better **thinking** than you have done before. Your thoughts will be constructive.

Hereafter, make it a point to relax—mentally, and physically—every time you can. Each time you have completed a task which required the expenditure of energy—relax a few moments to recapture it. While eating your lunch, **relax**. While waiting for a street car or bus—**relax**. Form the habit of automatically relaxing the moment the need of energy has passed. You'll reach a point where you and fatigue will be perfect strangers.

Should you at any time find difficulty becoming fully relaxed, literally talk to those parts of your body which are tense. If the muscles of your legs are tense,—talk to them. You are a mind with a body—and that body will obey you—if you **know** it will do so. You have but little patience with the mother who permits her small child to disobey instructions. Well, do not permit that body of yours to disobey your mental instructions.

## BETTER SLEEP THROUGH RELAXATION

You will no longer have difficulty in dropping off

in a peaceful, refreshing sleep, if you follow these simple instructions:

STEP 1. Do not use will-power in trying to go to sleep. The more you do so, the wider awake you will become. After retiring, just realize how good it feels to be in a comfortable bed with your clothing removed. Gain a "don't-care" attitude regarding sleep. Being comfortable and resting is the all important thing to keep in mind, as you'll agree.

STEP 2. Remove all cares of the day from your mind. There is nothing you can do about them while you are in bed,—so forget them until the morrow.

STEP 3. RELAX—mentally and physically. If necessary, talk to your mind and body—giving them instructions to relax. You will relax and you will go to sleep promptly—and when you awake in the morning, you will feel "on top of the world" and anxious to start an eventful day.

## KEEP YOUTHFUL THROUGH RELAXATION

In learning to relax,—do not forget the facial muscles. Most of the unpleasant expressions you find on faces, were put there through tenseness. The vertical lines between the eyes were put there when you wrinkled your forehead while thinking or working. The so-called crow's feet at the corners of the eyes were put there by squinting. Hard lines are carved around the mouth through anger and a bad disposition.

A smiling face is a relaxed face. You have heard much about the value of a smile so far as personality is concerned;—now you know that smiling will also enhance your beauty. So, do not forget to keep a pleasant smile on your face while you practice your relaxing exercises.

## BETTER HEALTH THROUGH RELAXATION

It would be possible to write a book of several hundred pages, outlining the many physical ailments and complications which can come to the person who is continually tense. The list could include indigestion; poor circulation; heart trouble; headaches; etc. It will be easy for you to understand how your health will improve in every way now that you are seriously developing the art of relaxation.

## EATING WHILE RELAXED

The only time one should eat is when relaxed. If you are under a mental or physical strain when meal time arrives; **skip your meal.** It will do far less harm to be hungry for a few hours, than to eat when the mind and body are tense.

Right here I might say a word about bad dispositions in addition to what was said in an earlier text. A person with a bad disposition invariably suffers from many physical ailments. Usually most fussing is done at meal time. The one with an unpleasant disposition will find fault with everything and every body. Food taken in the system under such conditions can not properly digest, with the result that the many ailments associated with indigestion will be experienced.

**The Law of Gravity**

Place a sack of flour in an upright position and it will soon bulge near the bottom. The law of gravity is at work. Human beings, from the time of birth, spend about two-thirds of each 24 hours in an upright-position—even when sitting. The law of gravity still works—and often the protruding "tummy" which we think of as being fat,—is nothing more than drooping organs—prolapses (a rather general female complaint). Many ailments, of which constipation is one, often result from drooping organs.

The Slant Board has been found to be a boon to both men and women. A fifteen-minute period on the Slant Board once or twice daily will put the law of gravity into reverse and cause the organs to fall back into their natural position.

The Slant Board is any board about 16-inches in width and at least 6-feet long. It is placed with one end resting on a chair, bed, couch—or on any solid object approximately 2-feet in height. Lie on this board—on your back—with your head down. Do so for periods of about fifteen minutes at a time, once or twice each day.

## SLANT BOARD FOR RELAXATION

You will find your board a great help in connection with relaxation. It is not at all difficult to relax while on the slant board. So, you can consider that, while you are so reclining, you are not only helping to promote health—but you are also helping nature to restore lost energy through this ideal relaxation.

## SLANT BOARD FOR HEALTH

The fluoroscope reveals an amazingly high percentage of people with drooping colons. This is another evidence of the work of the law of gravity. And with so many people affected with drooping colons, it is little wonder that there are so many people suffering from internal sluggishness-constipation!

The slant board will throw the law of gravity into reverse and cause it to work for you instead of against you. While using the board to relieve constipation, it is suggested that you gently massage the intestinal region with your hands. Also, draw your stomach in as far as possible.

## SLANT BOARD FOR BEAUTY

Would you like to have your face lifted? Well, the slant board will do it **for you,** in a most satisfactory manner. If your face and neck are showing age signs,—what do you see? The result of the law of gravity. The skin has become soft—and old man gravity has been pulling down. When you are on the slant board, look at yourself in a hand mirror. Notice—with pleasure—how gravity is encouraging the tissue of your neck and face up into its youngest and most line-free state.

As the tissue—and muscles—drop back into place, gravity is also bringing an additional supply of blood to that region, nourishing and strengthening your tissue and muscles, making it natural for them to remain where they belong.

If you ever have occasion to use a beauty mask, (beauty clay) the most ideal time is while you are reclining on the slant board.

Before applying the beauty mask, lie on the slant board a few minutes in order to relax the muscles and tissue of the face and neck so that they will naturally fall back to their origin place. Then apply the preparation—following the maker's instructions, of course.

## SLANT BOARD FOR BRAIN WORKERS

When you are mentally tired from study and thinking; you will find a few moments on the Slant Board will rest your brain so that you may resume your work with a clearer mind. Once a brain worker forms the habit of using the Slant Boar, he will find himself capable of far more—and better—mental work.

## EXERCISING ON THE SLANT BOARD

If you are following any routine of physical exercise—either for reducing or body building, you will be amazed to find how much more effective your exercises will be when you do them on the slant board—with your feet much higher than your head. With all of your organs in their proper place; through the law of gravity, it is easy to understand that your exercising will develop the strength to keep them where they belong.

*May Joy and Peace Be Yours!*

# InHABITing Pattern #9: A Reading
## *Habit*
### by Napoleon Hill

Now let us examine this word "habit"!

Webster's dictionary gives the word many definitions, among them: "Habit implies a settled disposition or tendency *due to repetition*; custom suggests the fact of repetition rather than the tendency to repeat; usage (applying only to a considerable body of people) adds the implication of long acceptation or standing; both custom and usage often suggest authority; as, we do many things mechanically from force of habit."

Webster's definition runs on into considerable additional detail, but no part of it comes within sight of describing the law that fixes all habits; this omission being due no doubt to the fact that the law of Cosmic Habitforce had not been revealed to the editors of this dictionary. But we observe one significant and important word in the Webster definition—the word "repetition." It is important because it describes the means by which any habit is begun.

The habit of Definiteness of Purpose, for example, becomes a habit only by repletion of the thought of that purpose, by bringing the thought into the mind repeatedly; by *repeatedly* submitting the thought to the imagination with a burning desire for its fulfillment, until the imagination creates a practical plan for attaining this desire; by applying the *habit* of Faith in connection with the desire, and doing it so intensely and repeatedly that one may see himself already in possession of the object of his desires, *even before he begins to attain it.*

The building of voluntary positive habits calls for the application of self-discipline, persistence, willpower and Faith, all of which are available to the person who has assimilated the sixteen preceding principles of this philosophy.

Voluntary habit-building is self-discipline in its highest and noblest form of application!

And all voluntary positive habits are the products of willpower directed toward the attainment of definite ends. *They originate with the individual*, not with Cosmic Habitforce. And they must be grounded in the mind through repetition of thoughts and deeds until they are taken over by Cosmic Habitforce and are given fixation, after which they operate automatically.

The word *habit* is an important word in connection with this philosophy of individual achievement, for it represents the real cause of every man's economic, social, professional, occupational and spiritual condition in life. We are where we are and what we are because of our fixed habits. And we may be where we wish to be and what we wish to be only by the development and maintenance of our *voluntary habits*.

Thus we see that this entire philosophy leads inevitably to an understanding and application of the law of Cosmic Habitforce—the power of fixation of all habits!

The major purpose of each of the sixteen preceding principles of this philosophy is that of aiding the individual in the development of a particular, specialized form of habit that is necessary as a means of enabling him to *take full possession of his own mind!* This too must become a habit!

Source: *The Master-Key to Riches*. Napoleon Hill. Willing Publishing Company. 1945. Pgs. 208-210.

## InHABITing Pattern #10: A Suggestion
*The Power to Choose*
by J. Martin Kohe

Man must realize that the most important thing in life is LIFE. Therefore, he owes his first duty to this LIFE which he possesses. If he takes care of his LIFE, it will be what he wants it to be. If he neglects his own LIFE . . . it will be what he does not want it to be. After the UNIVERSAL POWER gives man LIFE . . . then it is up to MAN TO CHOOSE TO DO WITH IT AS HE SEES FIT.

May we remind you of a poem we came across some time ago:

*"I shall pass through this world but once
Any good, therefore, that I can do,
Or any kindness that I can show*

## TEXT NO. 5 - PHYSICAL WELLNESS AND TENSENESS

*To any human being,*
*Let me do it now. Let me*
*Not defer it or neglect it,*
*For I shall not pass this way again."*

— Henry Drummond

Therefore, the fact remains that inasmuch as we are going through life JUST ONCE we should choose to make life a confident one, instead of a timid one . . . that we should choose to make a calm life rather than one of restlessness . . . that we should choose to have poise rather than confusion . . . that we should choose to make the most of life for ourselves and everyone else around us . . . rather than spoil our own lives and those about us. We have the POWER TO CHOOSE . . . LET US USE IT TO THE BEST OF OUR ABILITY. As we use our own minds to CHOOSE THE BEST so we will find that the UNIVERSAL MIND will come to our aid and assistance to help us choose the BEST. Together we cannot fail. WE MUST SUCCEED!

Source: *Your Greatest Power*. J. Martin Kohe. Success Unlimited, Inc. 1953. Pgs. 59-61.

# TEXT No. 6

# SELF-MASTERY

ABOUT the year 400 B.C., Socrates, the Grecian sage and teacher, uttered two words which have probably been quoted more than any other two words in our vocabulary: "Know Thyself." It is highly desirable that we do know ourselves, and I have often urged my students to follow the advice of this great man. But, to merely know ourselves is not enough. We must go a step further and **master ourselves.** Knowing ourselves, of course, means just that, knowing both the good and the bad traits. And, sometimes, when we do know ourselves—we lose so much self respect, we have no incentive to do anything which could contribute to our well being. So, I will be bold enough to say that by merely knowing one's self can be just as damaging as it could be constructive.

Students of the **Magic Formula** are advised to know themselves for a specific purpose. They are urged to examine themselves in the same spirit an auditor would use in checking the books of a business concern;—to uncover assets and liabilities. After an audit is completed and the report lies on the chief's desk,—what does he do with it? Does he just take the figures for granted as revealing an unchangeable picture? No, not if he is a good executive. He will study the statement with the view to eliminate as many liabilities as possible, and enlarge on the assets. Such a procedure is the one which will spell growth. In other words, the auditor, in a Socratic **"Know Thyself"** way, will paint a picture of the business as is;—the executive will endeavor to profit by the picture and improve his business.

You are now ahead of me, I am sure. You now I am about to suggest that you first know yourself—then, from what you have learned, advise a plan of action which will enable you to enlarge on your assets—good qualities—and minimize your liabilities—undesirable qualities. And, of course, you are right.

Most people, without studying this or any other self-improvement course, know large numbers of things they can do to help themselves,—yet, but very few of them do them. Why? Because they have the feeling that to climb means giving up many of those things which now give pleasure, and in turn, doing things which are laborious, uninteresting and even boring. All of this, of course, is definitely wrong.

It has been my good fortune to associate with many men and women who were making great strides on the road to wealth and fame. I have found these people to be enthusiastic, energetic and **happy.** They are getting lots out of life. And they are not working nearly as hard as ne'er-do-wells who are always hiding behind alibies as to why they are not succeeding in life.

This text will deal with **self-mastery** in the same daring manner as the principles so far given in previous texts. You will begin NOW in being your own master,—then, as you progress, the understanding of the "why" will certainly be clear to you.

There are five steps to follow in gaining self-masterly. I will not emphasize the necessary of following through on these steps carefully and thoughtfully, because by now you know the great rewards which can come to you through the application of these basic principles.

**STEP 1.** The very first step one must take in gaining self-mastery is to have respect for himself. No man who has lost his self respect can ever expect to be master of himself.

It is tragic when we realize how many people are being held back through a loss of self respect. These individuals, either consciously or otherwise, feel they are not entitled to the good breaks in life, and they act accordingly. They might make feeble attempts to succeed and each time they fail—feel certain they were not meant to be happy or successful.

If you were called upon to forgive another for any wrong which has been done toward you, you would be happy to forgive, wouldn't you? You would forgive as cheerfully as you would look for forgiveness from others.

There is one person we never think of in connection with forgiveness—and that person is ourselves. At first it may seem strange to suggest that you forgive yourself,—but as you think of it you realize that your body is just as much a part of humanity as the body of another; and if it is right to forgive another,—it is equally right that you should forgive yourself. So, Step 1 in this text on Self Mastery is to cleanse your heart and soul of all semblances of ill will which you might have been holding against yourself. Know that it is human to err—that everyone has erred at some time and instead of being held back by your mistakes of the past, you will profit by them.

Before proceeding to Step 2, repeat the following affirmation slowly and thoughtfully: *I have cleansed my heart and mind of all consciousness of my mistakes of the past. I have grown through these mistakes and have learned how to better conduct myself in the future. So far as I can I will assist others in avoiding similar mistakes. I have the utmost respect for myself, knowing that my life ahead will be a glorious one and my conduct will merit the approval of all with whom I come in contact. For this I am humbly grateful.*

**STEP 2.** Meditate for a moment over the words "Self-Mastery." Analyze them! Think about them! What do they mean? Self-Mastery, just as the words imply, means mastering self. The one who masters himself, does the things he want to do and refrains from doing the things he does not want to do.

I implied before that many people shy from Self-Mastery, feeling that too many sacrifices are necessary. If you will reflect over the last sentence in the above paragraph, you'll find that this is not so. I said that the master will do the things he wants to do—and will refrain from doing the things he **does not want to do.** Is there any sacrifice there? Is it a sacrifice give up something you **do not want to do?** You see, after you become your own master, you form a definite dislike for the things which you have found to retard your progress, hurt your health, or destroy your happiness. For many years I was a very heavy smoker. I smoked just as long as I wanted to, regardless of the urging of my friends to do otherwise. I continued smoking, until I reached a point where I no longer wanted to smoke,—then I stopped. I also drank quite a bit. I was never a drunkard and was intoxicated but a few times,—but I did drink quite consistently which could have lead me to a dangerous state. Notwithstanding all the warnings regarding the ill effects of alcohol, I continued to drink so long as I wanted to. One day I had the feeling that I no longer wanted to drink,—so I quit because I desired to. Does this mean suffering? Certainly not. I was doing the things I wanted to do. At this point, I want to make it clear, I am not dictating to you regarding your habits. They are yours and you hold on to them as long as you want to. When the day comes that you will want to abandon your habits,—you'll do so as part of your Self-Mastery—and not because others influenced you to do so.

So, in Step 2 you are to reach a point of understanding whereby you will fully realize what it means to be master of self.

STEP 3. Do you remember Step 1 in the first Text? I hope so! It was DETERMINATION. In this step we make use of this determination in a very specific way. We determine to become our own master. So right now,—relax fully and then repeat the following s-l-o-w-l-y and thoughtfully. *"I am master of the thoughts I am thinking and the things I am doing. My future will be of my own making and will be a bright future, because I will do those things only which will assure a future of radiant health, prosperity and happiness."*

STEP 4. Take a sheet of paper and draw a line down the center of it. On the left half—list at least 10 things about yourself which you can consider as negative or destructive characteristics;—anything which you feel might be holding you back. On the right side list about ten of your desirable qualities;—those traits which you would like to retain and even add to. Give considerable thought as you make out this list. Select each item carefully. After you have your ten assets and ten liabilities,—study them as to the order of their importance.— You might take a fresh sheet of paper and rewrite the lists, putting down the most important items first; the worst trait first on the negative side—and the best trait first on the positive side, etc..

| TEXT 6 Assets | Liabilities |
|---|---|
| Good Natured | Worry |
| Friendly | Timid |
| Ambitious | Smoke |
| Fair Health | Poor Talker |
| Honest | Jealous |
| Reliable | Selfish |
| Clean | Argumentative |
| Alert | Complaining |
| Good Memory | Unfair |
| Fair Education | Inferiority |

*Specimen*

**STEP 5.** Gain a sort of a detached feeling toward yourself. As you study the list made in connection with Step 4, look at each item in the same light as you would consider instructions you might give to an employee or associate. You are learning to know yourself and you have **determined** to **master** yourself. This list constitutes the first organized instructions you will give to yourself. Don't go about this hastily. Calmly plan in your own mind exactly how you will attain each one of these objectives. I would suggest that you start with the negative side first, because each negative quality you eliminate,— represents a definite step toward self-improvement.

Here is an important instruction! Do not start on the elimination of any of these negative conditions until you get yourself in the frame of mind whereby you **know you will be master.** To try in a half hearted way is almost certain to spell defeat. You should be in the mood whereby you **want** to dissolve the condition which has been detrimental to you,—and you have the determination to do so.

Use your own judgment as to whether or not you should attempt the elimination of more than one negative at a time. Be guided entirely by your feelings. If you feel that you would succeed better by taking one negative at a time, do so. If you believe you can handle more than one—or even all—at a time—splendid! But remember!—Do not attempt more than you can carry through.

So far as the items on the positive side of your sheet are concerned, it will not require much special instruction from me. Look over the items and then, with that determination of yours all ready for the job—take the items—single or collectively—and determine to add to those desirable qualities.

At this point, I might suggest that you refer to Step 7 in the first Text. In this step you solve to show continuous progress. *"Every Day I'm On My Way."* This applies to what you have attained and gained in this text as much as it did in the former ones.

Under no circumstances leave this text until it has become a part of you. IT IS IMPORTANT, every word of it. Between now and the time you take up Text 7, spend a few minutes each day in re-reading this one. THINK AS YOU READ. Realize that, with the possession of **Self Mastery,** you can climb to great heights. You will find opportunities at every corner awaiting your invitation.

And, now—*May Joy and Peace Be Yours!*

"Ev'ry Day I'm On My Way."

## InHABITing Pattern #11:  A Suggestion
*Five Big Ways to Rise above Disaster*
by Dorothy Carnegie

1. Accept the inevitable and give time a chance.
2. Take action against trouble.
3. Concentrate on helping others.
4. Use all we have of life while we have it.
5. Count your blessings.

Source: ***Don't Grow Old–Grow Up!*** Dorothy Carnegie. E.P. Dutton & Co., Inc. 1956. Pg. 40.

## InHABITing Pattern #12:  A Reading
*Overcoming Environment*
by Orison Swett Marden

A Spanish proverb says that he who lives with wolves learns to howl.

Those who constantly associate with habitual failures, with the nobodies, with the slipshod, the lazy, the unambitious, those who have no great absorbing life-purpose, tend to become failures and nobodies themselves, for such people leave their indelible inferiority upon every life they touch.

Napoleon was superstitious about associating with failures. He would never have anything to do with an unlucky man. He was mortally afraid of people who had always been unsuccessful and had continually failed in their undertakings. He believed their influence was sinister.

It is infinitely easier to march with an army to inspiring music than to march alone. It is easier to keep up our standards, to keep our ideals bright and polished, when we are right in touch with others who are trying to do the same thing. Their enthusiasm and earnestness are contagious. How often we see a youth who has never seemed to amount to anything, who is lazy and has no aim, suddenly revolutionized by coming in contact with an ambition-arousing environment. Country boys sometimes first discover themselves when they go to the city. Some are aroused for the first time at school or college. In others, the spark of ambition is awakened by teachers or friends who understand them, and see in them what perhaps their parents had not seen themselves.

Source: *Success Fundamentals*. Orison Swett Marden. Thomas Y. Crowell Company. 1920. Pgs.145-146.

### TEXT No. 7

# THE REALM OF SUCCESS

MONEY is merely an idea! This statement will at once cause eye-brows to arch and questions to be asked. We look at money as something real. We take a dollar bill and hold it in our hands and feel that we have something substantial. In reality, so far as stable value is concerned—a piece of money is as flexible as a rubber band.

To illustrate the statement just made; suppose potatoes were sold at $1 per bushel. Your dollar would be worth $1 so far as a bushel of potatoes is concerned. Now then, imagine potatoes rising in price to $2 per bushel, your dollar bill would then be worth only 50 cents compared to the price of potatoes. This will apply to the purchase of anything. The worth of your dollar depends entirely upon the value which is placed on the commodity you buy.

This, however, does not back up the first statement made to the effect that money is only an idea;—so let's prove it. Suppose there were 10 people in a room and only one has any money, and he has but $1. We will call him Man No. 1. All right,—Man No. 2 has a pocket knife he is willing to sell to Man No. 1 for $1 and this man buys it, giving his dollar to Man No. 2. Man No. 3 has a book which Man No. 2 wants, so he buys it, giving his dollar to Man No. 3. This goes all around until Man No. 10 finally has the dollar and even he does not retain it. He buys something of Man No. 1 for a dollar,—and gives him back his original dollar. In this room $10 cash transactions have taken place with only $1 in currency.

This same principle holds good in commerce. In one year in the United States there were 150 billion dollars' worth of transactions with only 4 billion dollars in currency.

United States money is backed up by gold. For all the money printed or minted there must be equal value of gold stored in the government vaults. But the value placed on gold is manmade. It is not decreed by nature. At the time this is being written, the value of gold is $35 per ounce, and $35 worth of money can be minted for each ounce of gold in storage. Suppose, for example, the law makers in Washington wish to declare a value of $40 per ounce on our gold, then $5 of currency more could be coined every ounce of gold being held.

Suppose in some mysterious way the gold reserve of the United States should disappear and no one would know about it. We would continue to carry on with our currency bearing the same purchase value as it now has. Should the disappearance become known, then at once the money value would drop to nothing.

It is not my intention to enter into a discussion of economics,—I merely wished to make a point regarding the unreality of money. If you have followed the reasoning given so far, you will agree with me that money is not a material thing at all, but a means of exchange based on a nationally accepted idea.

It was pointed out that the price of gold was a man fixed valuation. This brings me to an interesting and, perhaps, unexpected question: "What value do you place on yourself?"

Our material worth is based entirely on the value we place on ourselves. If you value yourself at $75 per week and consider a modest home about as much as you can expect in life—you'll get no more because that is your appraisal of yourself. If you place a value of $250 per week on yourself and consider yourself entitled to a fine home,—and really mean it,—you'll be opening the way for just such conditions.

By now you have gained the impression that what happens to us in life is a reflection of the attitude we hold toward ourselves. And, before continuing further, make certain you understand what I mean by attitude. I do not mean the wish you hold regarding yourself. That will not help a particle. I mean the vision you have of yourself. Do you see yourself a success? If so, you're on your way toward being one. Do you see yourself a great power in your city, state or country? If so, you're on your way toward being one. Do you see yourself with a young and active body? If so, you are helping nature to produce just such a body.

The dominant idea in this text is to begin a process of conditioning of the Creative Mind for success. Three steps are to be followed and a period of six days will be allowed fixing these steps in your mind.

**STEP 1.** For the next two days, every time you think of it, repeat to yourself: **I CAN be a Success.** Motion creates emotion, you know, and the more you repeat these words the more you will realize you **CAN** be a success. And this is important! Most people who are not successful do not know this truth. They have not learned they can be a success. And, it is absolutely necessary that one knows he **CAN** be a success before he will actually become so. When you first open your eyes in the morning repeat these magical words. Many, many times during the day do so. And, by all means, when retiring at night go to sleep with the words fixed in your mind.

**STEP 2.** Starting on the third day and continuing for two days, repeat to yourself—frequently—**I WILL be a Success.** Merely knowing you can be a success, as you now know, is not enough. You must use that determination you have been acquiring in declaring that you **WILL** be a success. There is no doubt in your mind that the sun will set at night and rise in the morning. When you declare to yourself that you **WILL** be a Success, be just as certain. Do not even question the statement. Tell yourself you **WILL** be a Success with the same nonchalant assurance you would use if saying to yourself: "Well, I guess I'll go to bed." If you follow through on this step as indicated, by the end the second day there'll be no doubt whatsoever in your mind as to your future success. YOU **WILL** be a SUCCESS.

**STEP 3.** When is a person a success? When he has his bills all paid? When he has $1000? When he has $100,000? When he has $1,000,000?

A man is a success the moment he gains the consciousness that he is a success. If you have money in the bank, you know you can write a check any time you wish to use your money. When you have a success consciousness, it is like money in the bank because you know if you want something you have what it takes with which to get it.

Now then, you spent two days in fixing the truth in your mind that you **CAN** be a Success, followed by your determination to BE a Success. All right, since you **CAN** be a Success and **WILL** be a Success—you can truthfully say YOU **ARE** A SUCCESS. So, for another two days, hold the thought: I **AM** a Success.

Repeat this time and time again from the moment you awaken in the morning until you retire at night.

Do not feel that by merely fixing in your mind you are a success, money will begin dropping from the heavens, and that Dame Opportunity will at once begin beating an anvil chorus on your door. This will not happen. But, and here is the glorious part of this routine: The moment your Creative Mind has accepted the thought you **ARE** a Success, you will assume an entirely different feeling than you have ever had before. You will know that the future will be of your own making and that with your new attitude it will be a thrilling future of accomplishment after accomplishment.

Being a success, your Creative Mind, with its independent reasoning faculties, will guide you to do the things which will manifest success to you. Your thoughts will be constructive. If there ever had been any doubt in your mind as to the realization of the objectives you decided upon while studying Text 4, that doubt is now dissolved. You will instinctively know that those objectives will be **yours** and that you will **know** what you should do in order to bring them into being.

Before bringing this text to a close, I want to make sure you do not misinterpret the intent in back of this study. Results, if you follow through as you should, will seem miraculous. But the study of this course will not create miracles. Permit me to explain:

There are many who scan through every newspaper

and magazine looking for the contests with great prizes; sums running into thousands of dollars—as well as prizes valued at considerable sums. They enter the contests and dream and dream of how wonderful it would be to receive the main prize—not realizing that their chances are **one** in a million or more. These same people will listen to all of the radio programs which offer enormous prizes, dreaming of the joy which would come should they be the lucky ones, yet their chances of so being are even less than when entering contests.

I have had people ask me if they could list prize winning as an objective—and if studying this course would help them to win prizes. My answer is always NO. And, this is being added to this text,—so that you will not ask the same question.

Frankly, I am happy that my answer is NO to such queries. I am happy that the Magic Formula does not create the magic which will enable people to obtain anything they wanted, without effort. The course would fail dismally in bringing to my students that most cherished of all prizes—happiness.

I have known children to come into this world, born in wealth. They have never known what it is to live in a home without many servants. They have never known what it is to be without high priced automobiles with chauffeurs. They have never known what it means to be without a large wardrobe of fine clothes. What can they possibly get which makes them happy—especially since they either **have** everything,—or **can** have everything they want?

If you could have anything you wanted by merely waving a magic wand of some kind, then **nothing** would be of interest to you.

Achievement brings the great thrills in life, getting things through your own efforts. The fun in playing a game comes from winning through the skill you use.—If you would win every game you played, you would lose interest in playing. You can study a game so that you will win more frequently than otherwise—and in that case, your thrill comes from the fact that through your own efforts you are winning often. If it were just through luck, you would not be nearly as joyful over winning.

The Magic Formula teaches you how to be more skillful in playing the game of life. Following through on the principles shows you how to climb to greater heights; how to be a leader; how to make friends and have people like you;—how to have better health and live longer—and most of all, it brings to you the priceless feeling of contentment and extreme happiness. And,—this happiness is yours because it is YOU who are responsible for your climb,—not I or anyone else.

You are now half-way in the study of the Magic Formula for Personal Accomplishment. Each text should have brought to you tremendous results—particularly **this** one. If you have followed all instructions, by now you should be facing a life more glorious than you have ever dared to picture in your dreams. If this is not fully true and you feel it due to your eagerness to advance with the lessons, and that you did not take time to do everything suggested;—why not start all over again? You will lose only seven weeks by doing so and your rewards will be so great!

By reviewing the previous texts, you will gain even more than you did when you first read them. Through your development, the principles will mean more to you than they did before. So good student,—unless you have reached that point of ecstasy where you are certain of a thrilling life ahead of you,—**for your own sake,** follow my advice and start all over again.

*May Joy and Peace Be Yours!*

## InHABITing Pattern #13: A Practice
*The R2 A2 Formula: How To Recognize, Relate, Assimilate and Apply Success Principles*
by Napoleon Hill

Your ability to recognize, relate, assimilate and use the PMA Principles will give you the power to open any door, meet any challenge, overcome any obstacle and achieve wealth, health, happiness and the true riches of life.

The PMA Science of Success Course is comprised of seventeen fundamental principles that have stood the test of time. They can be compared to an orchestra that is composed of different sections—strings, brass, woodwinds, and percussion—which complement each other and produce a melodious, full, and pleasant sound. Think of yourself as the maestro of your own orchestra of self-help principles. The ability to recognize, relate, assimilate and apply the PMA principles is your baton. Use it to blend all seventeen principles into a symphony of success—a meaningful and productive life.

Like any formula, the R2A2 formula is made up of individual parts. Let's analyze each ingredient.

**R** ecognize: to identify the principle, idea, or technique

**R** elate: to connect or join together; to establish a relationship to your own life

**A** ssimilate: to make similar or alike: to incorporate; to absorb; to become a part of your thinking and action

**A** pply: follow through and act upon

Each ingredient in the formula is important and has special meaning; when combined, they will lead you to success. By using the formula, you will be able to focus the spotlight on the Success Principles that directed and guided Napoleon Hill and many other successful people to achieve their objectives. The same principles will help you achieve your Definite Major Goals in Life.

### How To Develop The Habit Of Using The R2 A2 Formula

First of all, you need a mental success reflex, a trigger phrase that will immediately direct your mind when you recognize a success principle, idea or technique.

**Example**

**Recognize:** I recognize the principle, idea or technique that is being used. It helped someone else—I can see the results—and it will work for me if I use it. "That's for me!"

**Relate:** Ask yourself, "What will the success

principle, idea or technique do for me?" IMPORTANT: You must relate it to yourself. Start with the most important living person as far as you are concerned: YOU.

**Assimilate:** "How can I use principles, ideas or techniques to achieve my goals or solve my problems? How can I absorb them into my behavior so that they become a part of me? How can I develop a success habit—a success reflex so that the right thing will be done?"

**Apply:** "What action will I take?" "When am I going to start?" Ask yourself these important questions and then follow through with the self-starter: DO IT NOW! Yes, DO IT NOW!

The R2A2 formula should become so ingrained in your mind that you can recognize success principles, ideas, or techniques by listening to a sermon or an inspirational recording, reading a newspaper or magazine article or a self-help book, and by studying the lives of great men and women. **Remember: Develop and use your own success reflex by seeking ways to say "That's for me!"** . . .

Source: *PMA Science of Success*. Educational Edition. The Napoleon Hill Foundation. 1984. Pgs. x-xi.

# InHABITing Pattern #14: A Suggestion
*Success or Failure? You Decide*
by Erna Ferrell Grabe and Paul C. Ferrell

The person who habitually maintains a feeling of hope, expectancy and desire has a far better "chance," let us say, for success, than a person who is morbid and despondent. Those first-named attributes are contributing factors—but they are not sufficient in themselves to establish success. In reality, it is the sum total of a man's mental attitudes, as well as mental attributes, that makes his life a success or a failure.

Source: *The Sub-Conscious Speaks*. Erna Ferrell Grabe and Paul C. Ferrell. DeVorss & Co. 1932. Pg. 49.

## TEXT No. 8

## THE MAGIC WAND

By now you know this course has not been misnamed. If you have followed through on the suggestions as given, you will agree that this is a Magic Formula,—or at least results accruing come as if through magic. In this text you will be given a mental tool which will prove of such great help to you, you might like to call it your **Magic Wand**. Through the use of it, you will be able to assure yourself success in practically every undertaking.

At one time, in a Midwestern city, I was conducting a series of lectures to a group, largely made up of men engaged in the field of engineering. The principle about to be revealed to you was given. Enthusiasm mounted among these men with engineering minds, because, as they put it, it was the first time they had ever encountered a success formula based on sound engineering principles.

Sometimes, in arriving at a formula for success we must analyze failure to determine why we failed—and through the failure be able, perhaps, to discover why we failed and what might have been done to avoid failure. There are three major reasons for failure. The first one is a lack of a well defined objective. This may be a bit hard to understand in the beginning,—but as we think about it, it becomes quite clear. Many times one might be dissatisfied with his present lot and may take steps to improve conditions, but he is not sure of what he really wants. A hunter would not bag much game if he merely shot his gun in the direction where there may be wild birds or animals. Not likely. He waits until he sees what he wants and then he takes a very careful aim.

The second common reason for failure is lack of consideration of the obstacles which might stand between him and his goal. He may decide on what he really wants and might take steps toward obtaining it,—but after he makes the start, encounters obstacles he had not anticipated which blocks his progress and in many cases causes complete failure.

The third reason for frequent failure is faulty plan of action; a plan which did not take all of the obstacles into consideration, so when they were encountered— the plan failed.

Suppose a group of financiers should decide to put a new automobile on the market. What would they do? They wouldn't be satisfied with the mere thought they were going to build "a" car. No,—they would determine what kind of car they wished to build,— whether one in the high priced group, low priced—or in between. This might be considered as step number one, or the **objective**.

After the type of car has been decided upon, before starting the manufacture of the car, much thought would be given to all of the problems which must be solved in connection with the manufacture and sale of the car. Factory site would be considered;—equipment necessary, then availability of materials must be given consideration. But, manufacture is not the only problem by any means. The financial backers must be assured there is a market for the car and they would want to know how to approach it. So, a study of market conditions would be made, which includes a survey of all competition to contend with. All of this preliminary study and investigation might come under the head of step number two or the intermediates between the objectives and the **plan of action**.

In this case, the plan of action would include everything necessary to get into proper production—and also the sales and advertising procedure which would develop the markets uncovered in the original survey.

This illustration might seem rather involved and, on the surface, gives no indication of the value of the **Magic Wand** as used in connection with simple everyday objectives.

First of all, let us reduce this **Magic Wand** to a concrete principle,—then we will learn how to apply it in connection with all of our desires, whether they

be minor or major. The **Magic Wand** consists of:
1. **The Desire.** By this, I mean that which you want to possess or achieve. And, the desire must be specific—not general. Know exactly what it is you want. This might mean a better job;—a business of your own; friends, a husband or wife. In fact, the desire can include anything which you feel stands between you and your happiness.
2. **The Intermediates.** An intermediate means anything which might stand between you and your desire. Sometimes these intermediates might fall into the category of resistances or obstacles,—or, as was the case in the illustration already given, information which must be assembled before a plan of action can be evolved. This second section of the Magic Wand is perhaps the most important of all, because it is through ignoring some or all of the intermediates that there are so many failures.
3. **The Plan of Action.** By now you are ahead of me. You instinctively know that the plan of action is one which is based upon full consideration of all the intermediates.

If you will study any failure with which you are familiar, you are most likely to find that the failure resulted from not knowing all of the intermediates. In other words, the plan was incomplete. Action would be started and fail through lack of proper information, or when an unexpected obstacle would be encountered.

It is plain to see how such a plan as the one herein outlined will enhance the possibility of success and minimize that of failure.

It will be helpful to actually use this **Magic Wand** on a few imaginary desires:

Suppose, for example, your desire is to become a designer of modern homes. You have always been interested in houses and you believe you have the ability to create a house which will have many more desirable features than the present homes.

All right, let us handle this problem as an engineer would. I told you that a group of engineers highly approved of this **Magic Wand,** and this is why: It was handled in exactly the same manner an engineer would use in his profession. If he were called upon to design, let us say, a factory building,—what would he do? He would not sit at a desk with his feet on top, and while blowing smoke rings—design the building. No, he would work at his drafting board and with an array of instruments proceed to put his thoughts on paper. But, before he starts planning his structure,—he considers the intermediates which would include the condition of the land and what must be done before any building could be started. The ground might have to be leveled off; built up, or excavated. He does not charge his memory with any of the intermediates, but puts them down on paper so that he can study them. In fact he must consider each and every one of the intermediates before he can even begin to plan his structure.

So, following the course of the engineer, we will likewise list our intermediates so that, in developing a plan of action, we will be enabled to visualize every condition which must be considered.

Following the diagram you will notice that at the top I have listed as the Desire: "To Become a Designer of Homes." Under the head of Intermediates, I have included such items as "Lack of Knowledge;" "Lack of Experience;" "Lack of Time;" etc. Now, as you see these intermediates—notice how comparatively simple it is to build a plan of action which will include all of them. Were you to attempt to keep them all in mind, it would appear much more complicated. And, not only that, in attempting to build a plan of action without all of the intermediates before you, it would be so easy to neglect one or more of them, which would make your plan of action faulty and most likely to fail.

In classes where I have taught Creative Psychology, after illustrating this Magic Wand, students would often say: "That's fine for one who knows what he wants,—but what will you do when you do not know what you want?" This Magic Wand will prove to be magic in this case just as well as in others. Under such circumstances your desire is to have an objective isn't this right? All right, put it down as desire and proceed as before. List all of reasons—or intermediates, which have prevented you from having an objective. Undoubtedly you would think of many things you would like to do or have were you situated differently than you are. In that case, list those things which could be holding you as you are,—then you would be in a position to build a satisfactory plan of action enabling you to determine just what objective you would like.

There will be times when the Desire seems so great it would be impossible to attain it through the use of the Magic Wand. This is not so, of course, but to simplify the procedure, break major desire down into several minor desires. Then apply the Magic Wand to each minor desire, until you finally ascend to your major desire. For example, if your major desire was to obtain national distribution for a new product,—instead of thinking of it as a whole, you could take smaller territories as minor desires and expand until you attain your major desire or objective.

*May Joy and Peace Be Yours!*

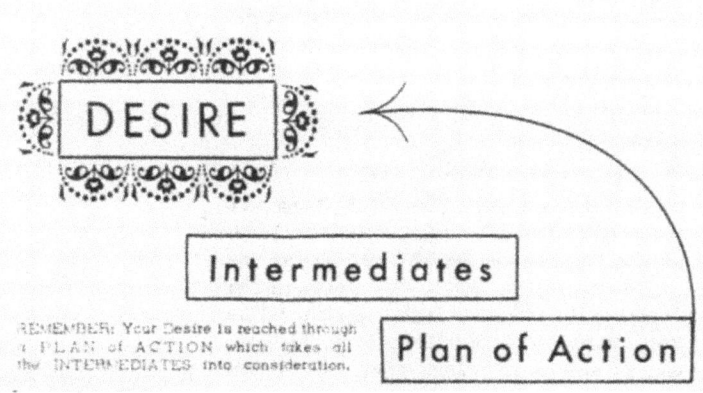

# PATTERNS FOR INHABITING SUCCESS

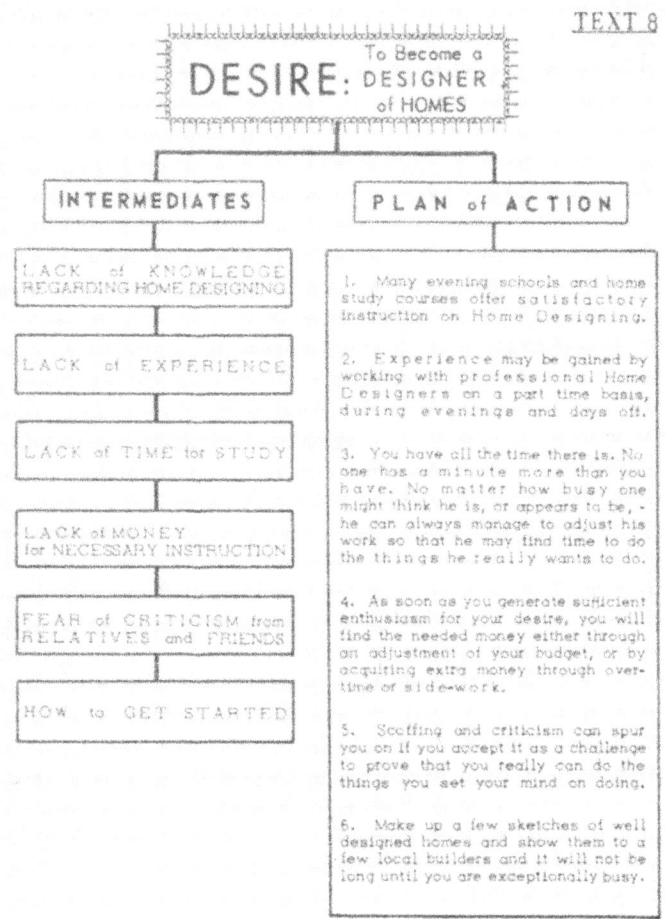

STUDY THIS DIAGRAM VERY CAREFULLY; THEN FILL OUT THE BLANK ON THE FOLLOWING PAGE; BASED ON ONE OF YOUR OWN DESIRES.

# TEXT NO. 8 - THE MAGIC WAND

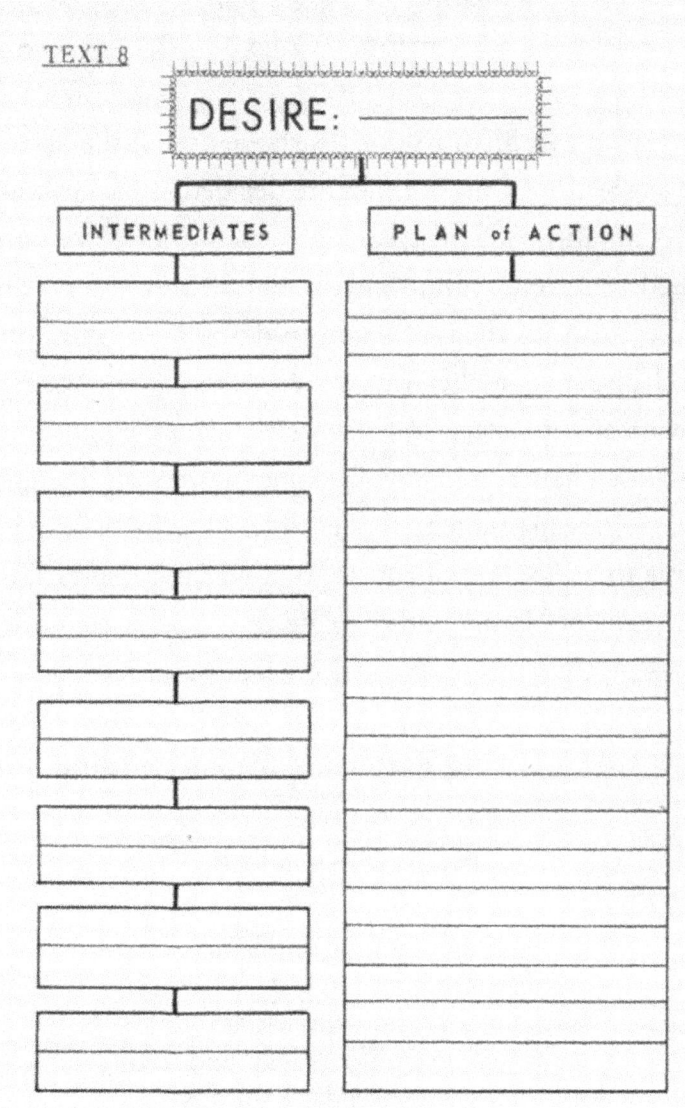

## InHABITing Pattern #15: A Reading
### *Slaves of Suggestion*
### by Emile Coué

From our birth to our death we are all the slaves of suggestion. Our destinies are decided by suggestion. It is an all-powerful tyrant of which, unless we take heed, we are the blind instruments. Now, it is in our power to turn the tables and to discipline suggestion, and direct it in the way we ourselves wish; then it becomes auto-suggestion: we have taken the reins into our own hands, and have become masters of the most marvelous instrument conceivable. Nothing is impossible to us, except, of course, that which is contrary to the laws of Nature and the Universe.

Source. *My Method*. Emile Coué. Doubleday, Page & Company. 1923. Pg. 6.

## InHABITing Pattern #16: A Reading
### *Habits*
### by Douglas Malloch

I saw a stream among the hills,
   Where any man might step across;
I saw it where the vale it fills,
   Where angry billows leap and toss;
And then I whispered, "I suppose
That so it is a habit grows."

Remember, always, will you, son,
   A habit grows as grows a stream?

Not suddenly a deed is done;
  We evil think, we evil dream,
Before we ever evil do;
  We form our habits, I and you.

Oh, let us rightly think and act
  While down the years we yet may look,
For age is like a cataract
  Any youth is like a running brook.
If you are on the evil side
Step back, before the stream grows wide.

Source. *Be The Best of Whatever You Are*. Douglas Malloch. The Scott Dowd Company. 1926. Pg. 19.

## TEXT No. 9

# PSYCHOLOGICAL COMPLEXES

TIMIDITY, worries, fears, phobias and complexes probably cause more pain and anguish than many of our severe physical ailments. If any of these destroyers of happiness are holding you back, this text will come to you bringing glad tidings.

"As the twig is bent, the tree will incline," we frequently hear,—and of course it is true. It might also be said that the psychological leanings of adults result from the way the mind is "bent" during childhood. Very few of these conditions are acquired after one reaches adulthood. Certain thoughts are implanted in the subconscious mind of a child which are carried on—and added to—into adulthood.

Consider timidity for a moment. How many adults can you think of who acquired it after reaching maturity? In all of my contacts with humanity, I have encountered but few timid individuals who became so in later life.

Thoughtless parents are usually the ones responsible for causing little Mary or John to develop into timid souls. To make this point clear: Mary knows a number of cute little songs and can sing them quite well. Guests arrive and mother proudly calls Mary into the room to show her off to the company. Mary is asked to sing one of her songs and might not feel inclined to do so at the time. Mother will declare: "I don't know what is the matter with Mary, she is so timid. When alone she will sing so much she becomes disturbing,—but when company comes,—she shuts up like a clam." Mother doesn't realize it, but she has given Mary a reputation to live up to. Mary, in order to be in keeping with mother's statement, must manifest timidity.

Later when Mary starts to school, she finds difficulty in talking before class and begins to discover she is not quite like other children. As she grows older, she finds a name for her condition;—**timidity.** She talks about it to other children, always saying she wished she was not so timid. We have learned that the thoughts we hold in our conscious mind are conveyed to our Creative mind which acts upon them. This means that every time we give expression to the thought: "I am timid"—we are making the condition that much more real. So on and on it goes: your thoughts of timidity continually make you more so.

Overcoming timidity is a simple matter if you will accept it as such. This statement may be a bit hard to believe at first, because timidity, throughout a lifetime, will cause so much mental suffering, it seems too good to be true that simple relief is at hand. But it is! Overcoming timidity is largely a matter of changing one's mind. For years you have been adding to your timidity through the thoughts of timidity you have been holding,—each one making your condition more apparent. To overcome timidity **all** that is necessary is to build up a consciousness just the **reverse** of the one you have. (Right now I am talking to the students who are timid. If it doesn't apply you, be happy,—but read this material just the same. It will help you to better understand others.) Right at this point I might warn you against using what I like to refer to as reverse positives. There are times when a positive can be negative in its effect. For example: To say: "I will not be timid," sounds like a positive statement,—and strictly speaking, it is a positive. But, it gives power to the existence of timidity. You do not want timidity—so forget it. Do not refer to it at all. All right, what do you want in place of timidity? You like to be with people. You like to talk to people. You like to help people? Right? Then, instead of declaring that you will free yourself of timidity, begin holding to the thought that you like people and like to be with them.

Whether you are timid or not,—it will prove of material help to repeat this statement; slowly and thoughtfully a number of times: *"I love all of humanity. I enjoy being with people. I like to converse with people. It gives me happiness to make others happy."*

As soon as this thought is fixed in your consciousness, your timidity will be gone, because you will not be timid in the presence of those you **like** to be with, and particularly since you love them all.

In treating yourself to overcome timidity, do not watch for results. Do not continue to observe whether or not you are less timid than you were before. Just take it for granted that the new consciousness you are developing is proving effectual and some day you'll awaken to the fact that you were timid—but that is all in the past. From this moment on, never again refer to yourself as being **timid,**—not even to yourself. If such a thought starts creeping into your mind,—erase it by repeating the resultful affirmation given above.

**Fear and phobias.** If you were to check these words in your dictionary you would find them to mean about the same,—except, perhaps, phobia is a **deep rooted** fear. One who is **fearful** will fear nearly everything: disease, death, accidents, panics, earthquakes, wars storms, etc. A phobia is usually a fear concentrated on a single object or class of objects; for example,—agoraphobia (fear of open spaces) claustrophobia (fear of closed places) dermatophobia (fear of diseases of the skin) doraphobia (fear of hides furs, etc.). There are a hundred or more different ones. Just as I mentioned in the previous chapter that timidity, in most cases, is acquired in childhood,—this is also true in connection with phobias. Most of them result from impressions imbedded in the Creative (subconscious) mind of the child. A friend of mine suffered from claustrophobia for years until he learned it had been caused by his mother who, instead of spanking him when naughty, would frighten him by threatening to lock him in a tight closet. Another person suffered from nictophobia (fear of darkness) because his mother, as punishment, would lock him in dark rooms "where the bugaboo would get him." A man went through a large portion of his life with a constant feeling that he was pursued,—that someone was creeping along beside him. A psychoanalyst uncovered the fact that, when this man was just a boy, a merchant caught him in the act of stealing apples from the barrel in front of his store, and frightened the lad by sneaking up in back of him and suddenly grabbing hold of him.

Fears and phobias can be quite successfully overcome through the use of reason. So far as fears are concerned,—do whatever your good judgment tells you to do as a measure of precaution, and then place your trust in God that everything will be all right. You know that your fear will do nothing except make you miserable and in some cases will actually attract that which is feared.

In considering fear, we should not confuse it with

**caution.** When a mother trains her young children to keep off the street, or refrain from playing with fire,—I do not think of that as being based on fear;—but, instead, the wise use of caution. I do not believe that to have insurance—life or fire—is an indication of fear,—but a sensible use of caution. But, after having used all precautionary measures, bring your mind to a state of peace. Maintaining a mind of fear will not prevent any of the feared conditions from happening;—but, on the contrary, will keep you in a state of confusion destroying all possibilities of happiness.

Phobias are often best treated through an understanding of the underlying causes,—and, to arrive at these causes will often require the services of a psychoanalyst.

A student of mine had suffered from zoophobia (fear of snakes and animals). She had such a fear of snakes she would not walk on grass fearing she might step on a snake. She shied from rocks and bushes, feeling a snake might strike at her. She was cured by making a study of snakes. She secured books from the library and learned much about reptiles of all kinds. She became so interested in them, she frequently visited the zoo so she could watch and study them. Her phobia had vanished.

As a treatment against fear, I suggest you use the following statement. Repeat it to yourself slowly and thoughtfully. Since everyone has fears to a certain extent, it would be advisable for each student to use this formula: —*"My Creative Mind is ever alert and keeps me safe from harm,—protecting me, and guiding me so that I may protect mine."*

**Worry.** You have already learned that the mind thinks in terms of pictures,—not words. In Text 4 you were told to keep before you a list of your objectives, those things—physical and material—which you want in life. You were told;—and now know to be true, that by holding mental pictures of **things you want**, you are putting forces to work toward bringing them into reality. Worry is the reverse of this procedure. You are holding mental pictures of things **you do NOT want.** Think about this a moment and you'll find it to be true. If you are worrying over financial troubles, you do not see yourself with a big bank-roll do you? No, you picture uneasy creditors, law-suits, collectors, etc. If you are worrying about an illness, you do not see yourself radiantly well, do you? No,—you visualize hospitals, operations, heavy expenses, etc. Am I not right?

Worrying never solves anything. Have you ever reached any successful solution to a problem through worry? Certainly not! Planning is constructive,—worry is destructive.

*Be glad you have problems!* To those of you who have been robbed of happiness through a multiplicity of problems (worries you have called them) will take issue with this statement. You will try to imagine how wonderful it would be to be absolutely free from all disturbing elements. Before you complete the study of this course you'll understand exactly what I mean. Right now,—try to visualize a condition where you had no problems of any kind. If you could have anything you want,—what would you want? Nothing would hold any interest. I lived in San Francisco for a number of years and during that time I never visited any of the world known points of interest in and around the Bay City, such as Mount Tamalpais; Twin Peaks; Fishman's Wharf, etc. I later went to New York where I stayed 14-years before paying a visit to my former home city. In a period of two weeks I saw more points of interest than I had formerly seen in the years of residence in San Francisco.

Here's a point I want you to think about—and always remember. It is not the problems which disturb us,—it is our lack of faith in our ability to solve them. I once coined a motto which has a humorous twist,— yet it is absolutely true: **Worry prevents our doing the very thing which would provide the means to prevent the worry.**

Would you like to have a sage always standing by your side ever ready to give you the answer to all problems which might arise? You would? Well, if you have been an attentive student, you know you have, in the form of your Creative Mind. You have learned that your Creative Mind with its great intelligence and vast reservoir of power is your faithful servant ready, willing and anxious to serve you at all times. So,—instead of worrying over a problem—which gets you exactly nowhere,—be happy that you are master of the situation and then instruct your mental self to give you the necessary guidance in solving the problem. Following is a typical instruction. If it doesn't fit your case, alter it so that it will. *"There is a solution to every problem. I will be guided to take the steps necessary to bring a satisfactory solution to...."* And, here you add the problem to which you are seeking a solution.

Here is something **IMPORTANT!** Keep your mind happy while working on your problems. To be gloomy, discouraged, despondent—is showing a lack of faith in your own Creative forces and will deter or even block the solution to the problem confronting you. I told you to be glad you have problems. After you once reach the point where your faith in yourself will bring the answer to your problems,—the feeling of mastery you will gain as you solve your problems will ever be a source of great satisfaction to you. And, speaking of mastery,—if you should by any means, have difficulty in accepting the truth of the statements contained in this text,—it might be well to stop now—right where you are and review Text 6 which deals with Self Mastery. Build up your consciousness of Self Mastery to the point where you will know you are bigger than the problems which confront you.

Can you imagine how it would feel to be bound, hand and foot, by chains which would give you no freedom of motion at all? And, can you also imagine how good it would feel to be released from those chains?

People who are held back through timidity, fear or worry, actually feel their hands are tied so far as freedom and happiness are concerned. For an entire week, before taking up the study of Text 10, I want you to actually sense a freedom through your release from any one or all of these psychological handicaps.

Under no circumstances permit fear or worry to enter your mind. If they persist, reread the portions of this text which refer to them. If timidity is the cross you have had to bear, gain a sense of happiness in knowing that it is being dissolved. And, if you do not feel you are making the improvement you have been expecting,—then reread the chapter on timidity in this text. It takes but a moment!

But, good student, this is **happy** week,—and I want you to be enthusiastically happy from morning until night—**all this week**. After a week of such routine it will begin to come natural to you—and you would not change for anything.

And now,—*May Joy and Peace Be Yours!*

# InHABITing Pattern #17: A Reading
## *The Golden Nugget*
### By Florence Scovel Shinn

A poor man was walking along a road when he met a traveler, who stopped him and said: "My good friend, I see you are poor. Take this gold nugget, sell it, and you will be rich all your days."

The man was overjoyed at his good fortune, and took the nugget home. He immediately found work and became so prosperous that he did not sell the nugget. Years passed, and he became a very rich man. One day he met a poor man on the road. He stopped him and said: "My good friend, I will give you this gold nugget, which, if you sell, will make you rich for life." The mendicant took the nugget, had it valued, and found it was only brass. So we see, the first man became rich through feeling rich, thinking the nugget was gold.

Every man has within himself a gold nugget; *it is his consciousness of gold, of opulence, which brings riches into his life.* In making his demands, man begins at his journey's end, that is, he declares *he has already received.* "Before ye call I shall answer."

Continually affirming establishes the belief in the subconscious.

Source: *The Writings of Florence Scovel Shinn.* The Game of Life and How to Play It. Florence Scovel Shinn. De Vorss & Company. 1988. Pgs. 82-83.

## InHABITing Pattern #18:  A Suggestion
*Thought Patterns*
by Ernest Holmes

It is a known fact that thoughts, often repeated, form patterns in mind which automatically reproduce themselves.  This is one of the basic principles of the new knowledge of the mind.  This illustration is often used by psychologists to explain continuously repeated neurotic conditions.  Why not use this creative law constructively, dislodging old thought patterns with their morbid reactions to life?  These thought patterns have hypnotized humanity into the belief that fear, unhappiness, poverty and sickness must prevail.  Why not disrobe this mental darkness with the glorious conception of the new light, now known to exist?  Say:

*My mind is open to new ideas.*

*The Spirit is ever active in me.*

*The Divine Mind is inexhaustible.*

*There is no weary or monotonous action in Spirit.*

*It is forever new and vibrant, fresh with ideas.*

*I know that I am continuously receiving new impressions from Life—new, better and fuller ways of living.*

*I let the newness, freshness and originality of Spirit permeate my entire consciousness.*

Source: *This Thing Called YOU.* Ernest Holmes. Putnam. 1997. Pgs. 35-36.

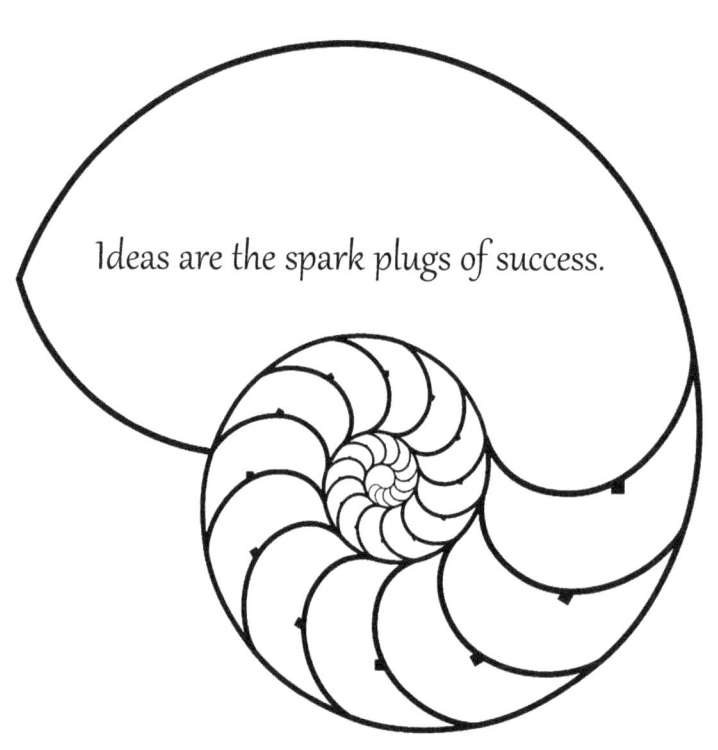
Ideas are the spark plugs of success.

## TEXT No. 10

# IDEAS—THE SPARK PLUGS OF SUCCESS

IDEAS are the spark plugs of success.

Fortunes, industry,—even empires have been built on ideas. Everything you buy is a projection of an idea. None of us will belittle the value of good constructive ideas, but the strange thing is, you will find very few people who have faith enough in themselves to give any value to their ideas.

"If that idea was any good, someone else would have thought of it." This expression has been used so many times, it is threadbare! Perhaps you have said it in the past,—but never again in the future, I am sure.

In the first part of this text I want to devote a bit of space to the value of ideas,—then I will end by showing you how to make your mind a veritable fountain of ideas.

A manufacturer of oil burners had advertised for a salesman. There was one young man who wanted the job very badly,—and he decided he would go after it constructively. The job offered was a good one,—so this chap knew there would be much competition. Before even approaching the company, he did a little investigating in the field in which he would be working, should he succeed in getting the position. He called on several users of the oil burner which he was hoping to handle. He asked them **why** they liked it. He visited many people using competitive oil burners—and asked them **why** they liked ones they were using. This young fellow took all of this information and put it in the form of a presentation. Then he went to the company and sent word to the sales manager to the effect that he felt he knew one of the reasons why he was not selling **more** of his oil burners. The sales manager was so interested in the report that it was presented to the board of directors along with certain recommendations. This young man landed the job in face of stiff competition and did so with the good will of all of the executives of the organization. That man had an **idea** and made use of it.

In a mid-western city, a young man wanted to obtain a position with one of the big advertising agencies. He knew that an ordinary solicitation for a position would not net him anything. He went to one of the executives and asked that he be given a desk and put to work for a week. At the end of the week the firm could determine whether or not he would prove to be a valuable man, and could fix its own value on his service for the trial week. The firm was so impressed with his sincerity, he was given a job. Today he is one of the officers of the company. He had an **idea** and made use of it.

A man opened a market in a small farming town. The community was so small he could not do more than make a scanty living if he had all of the towns business. He got a list of every person living within 35 miles of his store and started a mail campaign directing attention to all the fine things he had for them. He provided ample parking provisions and even a play yard for children. That man developed a business of over $300,000 per year,—more perhaps than all of the other merchants in that town put together. He had an **idea** and made use of it.

Every patent in the U.S. Patent Office is the result of an idea. Where did they come from? From whom did they come? A large percentage of them emanated from just plain folk—like you and me. In thinking of patents, it is often said that there are so many patents that it is increasingly difficult to think up something new. This, of course, is absolutely wrong. Each new patent issued opens up opportunities for countless more patents. An automobile is made up of thousands of different patents and each day sees new ideas coming into being regarding automotive transportation. With the invention of radio, an entirely new field of invention and discovery was opened up. Television has paved the way for countless hundreds of new inventions. So, as we think about it we realize that instead of opportunities for inventions decreasing—they are multiplying—rapidly.

Every time anything goes wrong, you are facing an opportunity for a new invention. The first can openers were gadgets which were inserted in the top of a can and pumped up and down—leaving a protruding saw-tooth edge around the top of the can. Many people, in opening a can would cut a finger; but would do nothing except, perhaps, say a few naughty words. One man, instead of feeling sorry for himself through a cut finger, asked himself why a can opener could not be made which would leave a smooth edge? He found no negative answer to this question, so went to work and invented an instrument which not only saved people from cutting themselves—but netted him a neat fortune in addition.

We might refer to ideas as crystallized thought; thought which has taken form; a foundation on which to build. Every place you look, you see ideas which have become realities. Every business is built on an idea. Everything you buy came from an idea. The clothes you wear, the house in which you live; the automobile you drive—all resulted from ideas.

You can struggle all your life without making much progress—when suddenly a single idea can lift you out of obscurity into the limelight of success and happiness.

There is no age limit to those who might develop ideas of value. In fact many people in the 60's, 70's and even beyond have conceived ideas which have enabled them to make more progress in a limited time than they had made throughout all of their previous years.

In my own personal case I might say that my greatest progress in life was after I had passed the 50-year mark. Age is often an advantage rather than otherwise. The knowledge one gains throughout the years "seasons" the mind, so that one may better evaluate his ideas.

I know I am right in assuming that you, the student now reading these lines, have within your mental equipment all that is necessary to enable you to develop ideas which will be of definite value to humanity, but which will also reap handsome rewards for you. Following are five steps which will help you to bring valuable ideas into being. Read them thoughtfully.

**STEP 1.** Before we can do anything, we must **know** that we can do it. This is just as true with the formulation of ideas as it is to the making of any tangible object. So, this being true, we must begin by **knowing** that we are fully capable of conceiving ideas of definite value. We have already learned through our **Magic Formula** that the proper way to create an **awareness** of any truth is by so instructing the mental self through the use of appropriate affirmations. The development of ideas will be no exception. Become thoroughly relaxed and repeat the following statement—and as you are doing so, sense the truth of every word you are expressing. *"My Mind is alert and active, continually bringing into consciousness a flow of constructive ideas of value to humanity."*

It might be well to commit this affirmation to

memory and whenever you are doing anything of a creative nature, repeat it to yourself.

Have you ever had a desire to become a writer? Would you like to have the ability to express yourself on paper? If so, before starting to write, repeat the affirmation and notice how fluid your thinking will be. Thoughts will flow to you as fast as you can record them.

A good conversationalist is one who has a faculty of expressing **ideas** in an interesting manner. Whenever you find yourself engaged in a conversation with others, you will find greater ease in conversing if you will repeat the affirmation to yourself, adding, perhaps, the thought: *"and I will find ease in expressing my thoughts and ideas to others."*

**STEP 2.** The step just concluded will aid you in conditioning your mind so that you will be able to develop constructive ideas. The purpose of this step is to cause you to become **idea conscious.** Develop a "curious" mind. While I do not recommend that you become disgruntled with everything you see, I do suggest that you form a habit of thinking in terms of improvement. When you have contact with anything, think of it in terms of "What can be done to improve this, or make it better?"

If you are employed, study the work you are doing. How can it be done better? Faster? Approaching your work with such an attitude will make it far more enjoyable. The time will pass more quickly and pleasantly—and from your constructive thinking, ideas may come into being which will reward you handsomely for your greater interest. But do not approach your work in this manner solely from the selfish standpoint. Do so for the stimulation which comes to one when a job is well done. The less you work for a reward, the more certain it is to come to you.

**STEP 3.** The purpose of this text is to arouse you to the point of **knowing** you are capable of valuable ideas, and to show you how to the make the greatest use of them. The suggestion paramount in this step is that you weigh each idea coming into consciousness as to its practicality. In the beginning, some ideas presenting themselves to you may be born from wishful thinking. Your desire for a certain condition may bring into mind thoughts which, on the surface, may appear as happy solutions. Think through on the ideas, and, if after careful reflection, they appear sound and practical to you, put them into effect without delay.

Ideas may occur to you which will require effort on your part in putting them into operation. To others they could offer opportunities for procrastination, but **not** with **you**. With your determination and **self-mastery,** that which may appear as labor to another will be welcomed by you, because it means growth and achievement.

**STEP 4.** An idea becomes something tangible the moment you do something about it. In the past, many worth-while ideas have flowed through your mind just as so much water will run under a bridge. An idea has its greatest intensity at the time of its birth. Preserve it before it begins to fade. Start an idea file. Each time an idea comes into your consciousness, unless you are so situated that you can make use of it at once, write it down. Write down everything which comes into mind regarding that idea. The very act of writing it down gives life to the idea and prevents it from fading. If the idea can be pictured, and you are at all adept with a pencil, make a sketch of it. Remember, the more you do regarding the idea, the bigger it grows and the more likely you are to do something about it. It will be well to review the ideas in your file at intervals to keep them alive in your mind. Also, should you gain thoughts which apply to ideas already in your idea file—be certain to record those thoughts, too.

**STEP 5.** A dormant idea is of no value. It is like having a surplus of food which is spoiling, while many people are starving.

The average mind is capable of conceiving far more valuable ideas than any one individual can make use of. To hoard ideas merely in hope that someday they may bring revenue to you is not too wise. Under such circumstances you are not gaining any compensation and humanity at large has failed to benefit through your creative forces. You will agree with this I am sure.

The more we give in life, the more we get. This is true regarding ideas. The moment we can establish the fact that we have valuable ideas, we will be called upon from various sources for our ideas. If an idea comes to you which you cannot make use of at the moment,—why not give it to the individual or firm who can use it? You will be amazed at the rewards which will come to you as a result of your generosity.

You might think of a way that a certain product can be improved. If you are not in a position to use the idea, why not present it to some manufacturer of that product? After you find your ideas are being used, you will have more confidence in yourself and, as a result, more, and perhaps even better, ideas will flow to you.

There are two things I want you to do before taking up the study of Text 11. The material given in this text is so valuable, I want you to make the most of it. Review Text 6 which covers **Self Mastery,** then re-read this text. With what you gained from the first reading—and then with the spirit which Text 6 will create, you will gain a great deal more from this text than you might at first have imagined.

Ideas are the seeds from which all accomplishments grow. Remember, **you have splendid ideas,** there are none better. Stay with this text until you are fully aware of this fact.

*May Joy and Peace Be Yours!*

## InHABITing Pattern #19: A Reading
*The Value of Versatility*
by Walter Pitkin

The versatile man develops habits in many fields. He reads Latin, handles wood working machinery, sails a boat, plays poker, has sold automobiles and phonographs, knows geography through and through, writes passable sonnets when in the mood, and runs a small greenhouse. Each skill deals with matters considerably removed from all others in the list. Now, it is well known that habits can be transferred to new situations in so far as the latter resemble those in which the habits were first formed. Thus, mastery of French aids one in learning Spanish only in so far as Spanish words, grammar, and style resemble French. In this case the aid would prove substantial; but of course the reverse would be true of skill in navigating, for in this there is no single factor that can be found in the use of Spanish. Each skill lies at the center of a field of possible activities. The closer the latter are to the center, the greater the ease of transferring that central skill to them. We might well call such a field a sphere of influence. At its outer edges the activities contain *only one factor each* in common with the focal skill. This represents the minimum of transfer.

Source: *More Power to You!* Walter Pitkin. Simon and Schuster. 1933. Pgs. 248-249.

## InHABITing Pattern #20: A Meditation
### *Your Life's Pattern*
### by Ben Sweetland

YOU ARE WHAT YOU THINK YOU ARE! As I say this, I am not implying that you like the condition in which you find yourself. No, you *would* like to be different, but you have remained as you are—because you have *seen* yourself *as you are*. The habits you have, which you would have liked to overcome, are with you, because you have not been able to see yourself without them. Perhaps your health is not better than it is, because you have never raised your vision to that point where you have *seen* yourself as being successful. You have not reached a state of supreme happiness, because complete happiness has not yet become a part of your consciousness.

Source: *I Can!* Ben Sweetland. Cadillac Publishing Company, Inc. 1953. Pgs. 37-38.

**The POWER which influences people. You possess the stuff from which leaders are made. You now learn how to use it.**

We might be dominated by others and do their bidding through fear,—but we follow a leader through choice.

# TEXT No. 11

# LEADERSHIP

THIS text will be so vitally important, I urge you not to begin it unless you are comfortably relaxed and have sufficient time to read it slowly and thoughtfully.

Frequently, in our haste to "see what it's all about," we will scan through a piece of literature hastily, just to get the gist of the ideas presented. That may be all right so far as fiction is concerned, but it is definitely not recommended for this work. In scanning, it is too easy to misinterpret a thought which will cause us to lose much of the value of the material presented. So, get yourself in the proper mood for a leisurely, enjoyable, profitable half-hour with this text.

**Influencing People.** The secret desire of most of us is to reach that point where we possess sufficient personal power to influence people and cause them to follow our dictates. Many books and courses on self improvement promise the student that he will soon possess that magnetic quality.

You are a person—a part of the people; what influences you? Let us strip this subject of all mystery and get right down to bare fundamentals. Why are some people outstanding so far as you are concerned? The same basic reason which causes children to gather around a candy shop window. Some people are attractive to you because they display qualities which you like. There is no magic; no force; no power. It is a law of attraction;—not in a magnetic sense, but due to the fact that through that person you see the fulfillment of a desire. It may be his kindliness; his understanding; generosity; sympathy; sincerity—or one or more of several very desirable characteristics. Think about this a moment and you'll find it to be true. Think of those whom you like best and question yourself as to why you like them. You will find in every case that you like these people because in some way they satisfy a desire on your part. Right now you may think of an exception. Perhaps you can name a few people who are on the receiving end; people to whom you are rendering a service. In this regard it will still be easy to prove my first assertions were correct. A person with a strong parental instinct—and who has been denied children, may find great pleasure in mothering, or acting as a father to others, without even realizing the existence of such a motivating force.

Since we now have the answer as to why we like others,—we also have the answer to the question: "How can I cause others to like me?"

Before proceeding further with this text I would

like to suggest that you put it down for a few moments and mentally review what you learned in Text 9 on Timidity and then go back to Text 6 on Self-Mastery and recall the enthusiasm you developed as you studied that gripping end fascinating subject.

In reaching that stage where you are an influence among people, you want to be free from timidity and possess an optimum of self-mastery.

Our envy of those who possess the ability to influence people is what makes it seem difficult for us to do likewise. We attend a party and notice there is always some one figure who seems to occupy the center of attention. At lodge or club meetings, there will be those who seem to be favored. What is the secret? The answer is simple. We like those who help us mentally, physically or financially. You might not wholly agree—at first—but as you think about it,—you will, wholeheartedly.

In this text, I will list many of the qualities which give us leadership, but there is one thing you must do first of all;—you must gain a **consciousness of leadership**. Perhaps up to now you have never seen yourself as one who can or does influence people. From this moment onward you must think of yourself as a person of influence—and, as this consciousness becomes definite, you will sense a difference in your home,—among your neighbors, friends, business associates,—everyone with whom you come in contact. As an assistance in gaining a consciousness of leadership,—it will be beneficial to repeat the following statement many times, and, until it becomes a part of you repeat it just before becoming a part of any like **group**. *"I like all people and enjoy doing everything I can to give happiness to those with whom I come in contact."* This affirmation might not appear to bear any relation to leadership,—but the real leaders are those who serve best. As you repeat this statement—back it up with the proper kind of mental pictures. See yourself as being popular,—not lonely and **wishing** you were popular. Create pictures of yourself as holding general interest when you are in a group. See yourself with an ever widening circle of friends. When you step into a room with other people, sense your leadership. This, you know, does not mean being "high hat," it means being gracious, responsive, vibrantly alive.

Before offering the formula for leadership there is a point I wish to make clear. Do not confuse leadership with dominance. We might be dominated by others and do their bidding through fear,—but we follow a leader through choice. To lead does not mean to dominate. Do you appreciate the difference?

As has been the practice in previous texts, the routine to be followed in developing leadership will be given to you in steps. Under no circumstance leave a step before you thoroughly understand and accept it. Doing this might slow your progress a bit,—but in gaining the great benefits to be derived from your **Magic Formula,** it is wise to make haste slowly.

**STEP 1. Like people.** Like all people. This is the most important step of all. Until you form a genuine liking for people,—you cannot expect to have people like you. You cannot conceal your feelings toward others;—they can sense it. Can't you tell whether or not a person likes you? Certainly you can. Well, others are just like you are in this respect. They sense whether or not you like them. Perhaps it may be a bit unnatural to like all people. Up to now you might have been a bit critical of others. Well, until it becomes natural to like all people, repeat and repeat the affirmation to the effect that you do like people. Motion creates emotion—and after you have made the statement enough times you will find that you have grown to like people.

You will think of many people who are on the bad side and therefore you cannot form an attachment for them. Yes you can! There is more good than bad in the worst of us. You do not have to like the bad in people. Like them because they are brothers and sisters in the big divine scheme of things and that it is unfortunate they have acquired or developed any bad characteristics. Like them because they are human beings and hope that in some way you will be able to assist them in overcoming their undesirable traits.

Hatred is a poison which actually affects us physically. It harms no one except those maintaining it. And, just as we can sense those who like us,—so too can we sense those who have hearts of hatred. If there have been people you have hated, do everything you can to win their friendship. Do it because it will help you by removing the hatred from your system. In cases where the hatred is so deep rooted you cannot rout it through mere words,—find something you can do for the one you have hated and see how quickly your hatred will disappear.

**STEP 2. Show an interest in people.** A philosopher once said: "The greatest thing in the world to me is me." This, of course, is true. Remember this when you are with others. Develop a **you attitude.** Think in terms of service to the other fellow. Point your conversation toward him and the things he likes. In the early part of this text you were told that you liked people who satisfied one or more of your desires. You will now begin to see the truth of this statement. Suppose you had been away on a trip and upon returning should meet an acquaintance who would enthusiastically say: "Oh, I can hardly wait to hear all about that trip you have just made." Wouldn't it impress you? Wouldn't it make you just a mite closer to that person? Well, the reverse is also true. If you direct your interest to others, they will become closer to you.

**STEP 3. Be generous with compliments.** Compliments do for one's personality what magnetism will do for a magnet. Upon opening a conversation with another, start out with a compliment and see how much closer it brings him to you. And it is so easy to do. You can find a reason for a compliment regarding everyone with whom you may come in contact. And remember, a compliment is **not** flattery. It is merited praise. You can compliment one on his health, his apparel, his appearance, alertness and the progress he is making in his job or business; his home, garden, car;—oh, there are so many things. But, make it a habit to open your conversation with a sincere compliment.

It is so natural for us to be self centered and think only of ourselves, it will take an effort on our part to form the habit of complimenting; so **work at it**. Think about compliments. Look for opportunities to extend them. It will pay you such handsome dividends. You'll be amazed to see how your circle of friends will grow.

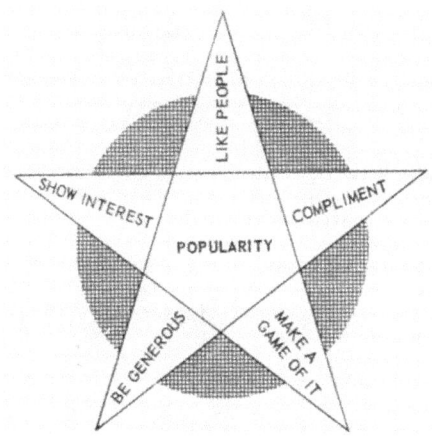

**STEP 4. Be generous.** There are more ways of being generous than by merely lending or giving money. In

fact, sometimes it is not even wise to give or lend money. There are many, many ways of being generous which would mean even more than money. You can share your knowledge and the fruits of your experience. You can share your friends. And, perhaps, the most valuable gift you can give is your friendship which really means your unspoken pledge to defend and protect under all circumstances. To have a friend—be a friend.

Many people, when meeting someone for the first time will think of the advantages—from a selfish standpoint—which might come from knowing that person. To you, who are now on your way to leadership, this will never enter your mind. As you meet strangers, your thoughts will be on the many things you might do which will be enjoyed and appreciated by him. Some might question the wisdom of such policy feeling that there is no fun in always being on the giving side. There is a surprise in store for such people if they will follow the advise given in this text. When we are finding our happiness by making other people happy,—they will begin looking for the same type of happiness and will show a distinct interest in you.

**STEP 5. Make a game of making friends.** When playing a game of any kind, you get a thrill when you win, don't you? Certainly! The thrill you get in winning a game, however, is nothing to the thrill which comes each time you make a friend. So, actually approach your newly developed leadership in the spirit of a game. Consciously go about making friends of those with whom you come in contact. And, the more difficult it is to "get under the skin" of the individual, the greater will be your victory when you do make a friend of him.

A saleslady in a department store was always exhausted at the end of the day and was seldom in a good mood. She complained of the task of trying to please unreasonable customers all day long. She was told to exert a conscious effort to make a friend of everyone she served. She did and became so enthusiastic over her work she did not like to see the days come to an end and would be eager to return to her work in the morning. Her reward came as customers began to call for her by name and her manager, in order to keep her happy, offered her a handsome increase in salary.

A salesman sells himself before he sells his product. If he will practice the rules given in this text his sales will increase because his number of friends will increase.

Business men will attract more customers if they will practice these principles because we like to deal with those who show an interest in more than the money we spend.

**Everyone** will benefit through the thoughts given in this text.

You might not aspire to be a leader from the standpoint of becoming a city, state or national official. But you are interested in processing that type of leadership which will give you poise and self-assurance in any gathering. This text will give it to you. In fact, it will enable you to climb to the specific objective you have set for yourself.

And now,—*May Joy and Peace Be Yours!*

## InHABITing Pattern #21: A Practice
*Dismiss the Rubbish*
by Frederick Pierce

The first thing to do in examining the mechanisms and the possibilities of autosuggestion is to dismiss from our minds as completely as possible whatever rubbish we may chance to have accumulated there from the writings of professional optimists. The quack is an ever-present phenomenon, common to all climates. The suggestion-quack assures us that we have only to think money and we shall be rich, to think fame and we shall be famous, to go about declaring that everything is all right, and everything will be all right. Unfortunately, what he says is not true, but he usually gets a considerable following because there is a natural tendency to seek a short cut and a side door into the kingdom of successful living. Knowledge involves study, and thorough study requires patient, persistent, hard work. Moreover, the acquirement of accurate knowledge might completely upset the professional optimist's quack philosophy. He finds it easier to hurdle such trifling obstacles as physiological and psychological facts, with the help of such catch phrases as, "he can who thinks he can," "right thinking makes right living," "a cheerful mind makes a sound body," and the like. The serious research worker can spare little time for such literature but it often supplies an element of real humor. In a single paragraph of one widely circulated book of this sort there is the ridiculous confusion of autosuggestion with a conflict between Unconscious and Fore-conscious based on a psychic trauma of childhood.

Autosuggestion, applied with sound technique, has produced, and is producing highly valuable results. It has passed the experimental stage. At Nancy, and at the Rousseau Institute in Geneva, it is in daily clinical and pedagogical use under responsible scientific direction. It has proved its value and its possibilities of future development. But unless applied in the right way it is useless.

Source: *Our Unconscious Mind*. Frederick Pierce. E.P. Dutton & Co., Inc. 1922. Pgs. 99-100.

## InHABITing Pattern #22:  A Reading
*Habit Tendencies*
by David Seabury

Science has proved that the old brain is the organism which directs a great percent of our automatic responses and primitive impulses, sensory and nervous reflexes, as well as some of the simpler inhibitory processes. At the same time it has no actual self-conscious thinking power. It can do no more than guide and protect an animal under average conditions through sense-awareness and inherited habit-reactions. Once we recognize, therefore, that habit is physiological and largely in the field of the lower brain, the dangers of habit building on a negative path become clear. Early environment which sets destructive pattern reaction in motion is actually the starting of the individual on a devolution back toward palaeolithic savagery. This is the criminal brought into being. By the very law of habit, which is never stationary, the individual moves to ever lower levels of action. A single tendency may remain through a lifetime, but each negative habit inclines to propagate a new one, just a little worse than itself. The man who persistently tells obscene stories and questionable jokes is likely to gradually lose his sense of what is decent humor, his idea of fun becomes ever more gross and sooner or later he seeks foul-mouthed associates.

Each series of reactions breeds acceptance of the neighboring type, until those become set and new patterns are in process of annexation. The negative path thus sweeps on and on, closing the life doors to other experiences and environments.

The positive path is equally productive of new habit formations. Each mass of affirmative habits creates sensitivity to the level above: nerves, gland and brain have become used to certain requirements and accept ever higher attenuations.

Source: *Unmasking Our Minds*. David Seabury. Boni and Liveright. 1924. Pgs. 269-270.

## TEXT No. 12

## GAINING A GOOD MEMORY

"I have forgotten." How many times do you use such an expression? Have you ever felt that your memory was fading, because you find it increasingly difficult to recall names and facts?

This text will be devoted to memory and how to develop a retentive one.

In an early text we learned that the mind of man has a portion above the level of consciousness which we refer to as the conscious mind and the portion below the level of consciousness we call the subconscious or Creative Mind.

The Creative Mind is the storehouse of memory,—and right now I will tell you something which may be a surprise to you. **The Creative Mind never forgets. Everything** you hear or read throughout your lifetime is retained in your Creative Mind. This has been proved so many times it is now an established fact. The dictionary says that to forget is to be unable to recall. If you will think about this for a moment you will gain a new concept of memory. To forget does not mean you no longer have the thought or idea. It merely means it has been misplaced, or has slipped from your conscious mind. The very fact that you do recall things to mind indicates that you have had the information all along, but at the moment it did not come into consciousness.

Already in this series of texts, you have, in several instances, learned how to give instructions to your mental self. And, if you have followed through on all suggestions so far made, you know your Creative Mind is ever responsive. It follows the dictates of the conscious mind, without question,—whether the suggestions be positive or negative. Frequently we give our Creative Mind the type of instructions we do not want carried out,—not intentionally, of course; but every time we start a thought with the personal pronoun "I" it is an instruction to our Creative Mind.

Should you wish to recall a thought to mind and it does not come at once, what do we-say? Usually our statement is something to the effect: "I've forgotten," or "I can't remember." Probably, you are now ahead of me. Whether you are or not,—when you make the statement "I have forgotten" you are literally telling your mental self to do nothing about it. The next time you wish to recall any fact, reverse your usual method and make a positive declaration such as: "I will remember," or, "it will come to me in a moment."

This means: you are instructing your mental self to delve into your mental storehouse for the fact you want and bring it into consciousness—and, if you believe what you have said, it certainly will.

In the beginning I referred to a fading memory. If you have ever felt your memory has been fading, you can put your mind to rest right now, because **a memory does not fade**. To prove this, think back over your past for a moment. Think of that red dress or red necktie you wore to school. Has the red faded to pink? Or if you recall to mind a terrific explosion you heard when a child, has that faded down to a slight sound? No, the red you recall is as vivid a red as when you first saw it, and the explosion is as loud as when you first heard it. The memory does not fade. We might misplace portions of information, but that which we do bring into consciousness is as it was when we first obtained it.

All right, why do we show all indications of a bad—or fading memory, if we never lose any knowledge we might have gained? Here, too, you might be ahead of me. It is because you have allowed yourself to acquire a bad memory consciousness. You have been holding thoughts to the effect that you have a bad memory,—and as you now know, every time you say: "I have a bad memory" you are giving yourself mental instructions to make your memory bad.

An attempt to recall names is one reason why we

develop a bad memory consciousness. While we are introduced to a person our attention will not be on the name,—but on the person behind the name. We might be noticing the clothing, or features, or some mannerism. We did not give any thought to the name when mentioned and later when we wish to recall it, it appears to be gone, and we begin blaming ourselves for having a bad memory.

Another reason for the appearance of a bad memory is the mental confusion we frequently allow to exist. We do not keep our thoughts under control by allowing so many side currents of thought to enter the mind. Under such circumstances, the information we want does not readily flow into consciousness and we add to our bad memory by further comment on it.

Age also plays a part. For some reason we have accepted the thought that good memory and age do not go together. We expect, as the years roll by, our memories will regress,—and in most cases they do;—but, **it is not the age which causes it.** It is the bad memory consciousness we develop. We expect our memories to weaken.

I have laid out five simple steps for you to follow in gaining a retentive memory. "Make haste slowly" in going through these steps. Stay with each one until it becomes a part of you,—until there is no doubt whatsoever regarding the truth contained in the step.

# TEXT NO. 12 - GAINING A GOOD MEMORY

**STEP 1.** Repeat the following statement to yourself frequently,—until the truth of it is in no way questioned by your conscious mind. *"I have a good memory. My mind is orderly. I am master of my thoughts at all times. I can at will recall to consciousness any facts which may be stored within my mental storehouse."*

If you are one who has been seeing yourself as having a bad memory, a statement of this kind might seem rather contradictory. But, when you realize that your memory became bad through holding "bad memory" thoughts,—the only way to correct the condition will be through a reversal of your type of thinking.

Actually rejoice that you have a good memory. Be happy that your memory is serving you as it was intended to do.

**STEP 2.** In addition to developing a consciousness of a good memory, do everything you can to fix facts and figures in your mind. For example, when you are introduced to someone, instead of merely saying the customary: "I am pleased to meet you," repeat the name, such as: "I'm very happy to meet you, Mr. Throckmorton." If the name is not a usual one,—you can make it still more impressive if, after repeating it during the introduction, comment on it. Asking how the name is spelled has a tendency to fix it in your mind. If you have a friend of the same name, it often helps you to remember by making a mental association—between the name to be remembered and the person you know of the same name. Writing a name down will often help one to remember it—so on the first occasion, make it a point to **see** the name you have committed to memory. Do not do these things **instead** of that which was suggested in Step 1,—but as aids in developing a consciousness of good memory. As you find your mind clicking on all things, you will think of yourself as having a good memory with the result that it will be good.

**STEP 3.** Memory exercises will help materially in gaining a good-memory consciousness. A good exercise is to take a list of words, such as you find in a book on spelling. Read five of the words,—then close the book and repeat the five in the order in which they were given. After that becomes easy, take six words,—then seven, eight, and so on. Keep adding a word. You will be surprised to find out how quickly you will reach a point where you are going to be able to recall long lists of words. As you remember the words, do not look at it as any special feat, but just another evidence that you have a good memory,—in fact, it is natural for you to have a good memory.

A good memory game which the whole family and guests can play,—is to arrange about twenty five items of different kinds on a table, and then everyone must pass the table slowly looking over everything displayed on it. They then go into another room and write down as many items as they can remember. Some people will play such a game with the feeling, "I know I won't be able to remember many" and they will be right. Others will know that they will be able to remember most or, all of the items and they, too, will be correct. A hat check girl in a large hotel was known for her good memory. She did not use a hat check of any kind, yet remembered the correct owners of all the hats and coats entrusted with her. I asked her how she accounted for her good memory. She laughed and replied: "I don't know how I do it,—I just know that I can." Perhaps she did not realize the psychological truth she was uttering, when she said, "I just know I can do it." That's all we need in order to have a good memory;—just know we have one. It's another way of saying we have developed a good-memory consciousness.

Room clerks in hotels are notorious for their good memories. One of them called me by name five years after I had been a guest in the hotel, and even went so far as to tell me the room I occupied when first in the hotel. I asked him if he made any conscious effort to remember names of guests. He told me he did not. He just remembered. This man had a consciousness of a good memory and did not mar it through any negative thoughts, as most people do.

**STEP 4.** Information is received through all of our five senses; sight, hearing, smelling, tasting and feeling. For a moment, let us think of seeing and hearing. Psychologists have found that humans are divided into two groups so far as memory perception is concerned. There are those who remember what they **see** longer than what they **hear,**—and on the other side, those who will remember what they **hear** longer than what they **see.** The sight minded are called visualists, and the ear minded are called oralists or acousticons.

Determine to which group you may belong. You can readily do this by thinking back over the last several lectures you heard and trying to recall as much of the talks as possible. Then refer mentally to some of the recent books and magazine articles you read and see how much of them you remember. You will find that it will be easier for you to remember one group than the other. If you remember the lectures the best, you are an oralist. If you remember the books the best, you are a visualist.

If you are an oralist, take advantage of every opportunity of attending good lectures. If you are a visualist, then you will want to spend much time with the printed word.

Knowing whether you are an oralist or a visualist will help you to fix facts in your mind. If you want to make a clear mental record of any fact, and you are an oralist, repeat it aloud a few times. If you are a visualist, write it down so that you will see it.

The senses of smell, taste and touch will also help you to improve your memory. It is possible to recall tastes and odors, just, as it is possible to retain a memory as to how objects feel. This latter phase of remembering is called tactile memory. As your memory develops, you will not only be able to bring into consciousness the words representing the thought, but also the taste, odor and feel, if any.

STEP 5. Develop your powers of observation. We all see, but not all of us observe. We see to the extent of seeing what we are doing or where we are going, but we do not make a mental impression of what the eyes are seeing. It is amazing how much more interesting the world becomes as we form the habit of noticing everything within range of our sight. And, developing the powers of observation improves the memory.

One of the best means of learning to observe is to **think as you see.** Think about the things you do see. Think of the size, shape, texture, color, odor, etc.

Of course, forming a habit of this kind will help to make you a better conversationalist because you will have more things to talk about, but right now we are thinking of observation merely from the standpoint of improved memory.

Talking about the things you see and hear will also fix them in your mind. So the next time you are in conversation with others, mention some of the things which you have discovered due to your newly acquired powers of observation.

This text can be worth far more to you than the entire cost of the course. Do not treat it lightly. Read it and re-read it,—and most important of all—practice everything suggested.

The biggest point of all in connection with memory is that from this moment on **you have good memory.** You will never again use the expression that you have forgotten or can't think of certain things. You will take the positive stand of **knowing** the facts will return to your consciousness.

In your conversation give yourself credit for having a good memory. If the subject is brought up, be firm in the statement: "I have a good memory." And, mean it!

And now,—*May Joy and Peace Be Yours!*

## InHABITing Pattern #23: A Suggestion
*Do It Now!*
by W. Clement Stone

This accountant was the same man who the night before had had the courage to ask: "How can I get my subconscious mind to work for me?" And he had been told about setting goals, inspirational dissatisfaction, self-motivators, and the self-starter *Do it now!* He also learned that he must choose a specific immediate goal and start toward it. And he learned these things too:

1. You affect your subconscious mind by verbal repetition. The subconscious mind is particularly affected by self-suggestions given under an emotional strain, or given with emotion.
2. The greatest power man possesses is the power of prayer.

He listened. He took time for reflection. He related and assimilated the principles. He prayed sincerely, reverently, and humbly for divine guidance. He believed he would receive it, and because he believed, he did receive it. And when he did, he didn't forget to give a sincere prayer of thanks.

Source: *The Success System That Never Fails.* W. Clement Stone. Prentice-Hall, Inc. 1962. Pgs. 76-77.

## InHABITing Pattern #24: A Meditation
### *Habits of Growth*
### by Napoleon Hill

The whole purpose of education, or so it should be at least, is to start the mind of the individual to growing and developing *from within*; to cause the mind to evolve and expand through constant changes in the thinking processes, so that the individual may eventually become acquainted with his own potential powers and thereby be capable of solving his personal problems.

Evidence that this theory conforms with nature's plans may be found in the fact that the better educated people of all times are those who graduate from the great UNIVERSITY OF HARD KNOCKS, through experiences *which force them to develop and use their mind-power.*

The law of change is one of the greatest of all sources of education! Understand this truth and you will no longer oppose the changes which give you a wider scope of understanding of yourself and the world at large. And you will no longer resist nature's breaking up of some of the habits you have formed *which have not brought you peace of mind or material riches.*

The traits the Creator most emphatically frowns upon in human beings are complacency, self-satisfaction, procrastination, fear and self-imposed limitations, all of which carry heavy penalties which are exacted from those who indulge such traits.

Through the law of change, man is forced to keep on growing. Whenever a nation, a business institution, or an individual, ceases to change and settles into a rut of routine habits, some mysterious power enters and smashes the setup, breaks up the old habits, lays the foundation for new and better habits.

*In everything and everyone the law of growth is through eternal change!*

Source: *You Can Work Your Own Miracles.* Random House. 1996. Pgs. 29-30.

## TEXT No. 13

# MASTER OF YOUR OWN DESTINY

EVEN those people who claim they are not superstitious will often wince a bit when they're confronted with the number 13. Throughout our entire lives we have heard so much about the bad luck associated with this number, it is difficult for most of us to be nonchalant when we're faced with 13. You will find those who bravely proclaim that 13 means nothing to them,—yet most of them—secretly, shy from it.

Naturally there is an origin to every superstition. The superstition regarding 13, according to legend, dates back to the Lord's Supper, where 13 sat at the table and one of them betrayed the Master.

This is Text 13, and I am going to make it a **Lucky 13**. And, there is no reason why a number can't be lucky as well as unlucky. 13 will prove a lucky number if you believe it as strongly as you might believe it to be unlucky.

What is luck? Webster says it is something which happens to one by chance. If this is true, then superstitions play no part in luck, because, according to the superstitious, when you do certain things, you obtain certain results. If you select the number 13, you will have bad luck. If you permit a black cat to cross your path, you will have bad luck. According to this belief, you have a certain control over what happens, because, by avoiding 13's, black cats, etc., you avoid bad luck. Also, the superstitious have omens which indicate good luck, such as 4-leaf clovers, rabbit's feet, etc. Then, by the same token, we can likewise control the condition, which might fall into this category thereby assuring ourselves good luck. Therefore, it would seem that since we can control the good things and bad things,—according to the true definition of luck—as being something which happens to one by chance, luck plays no part in superstition.

There are a certain number of things, beyond our control, which are daily happening to all of us. Some of these happenings appear to be good, others bad. To put it in the simple language of the street,—we are all subject to a certain number of good and bad breaks. But,—and here's an important point—the attitude we take toward "breaks" has a most definite influence on our futures.

If we have a negative consciousness, we will enlarge on the bad breaks to such an extent, we will be controlled by them. We will take a failure attitude toward ourselves and find it hard to do anything of a constructive nature. Our health becomes affected. We become gloomy and morbid. We have but few friends,—in short, life holds little to look forward to.

If we have a positive consciousness, the reverse is true. We magnify our good breaks to such an extent we are controlled by them. We become more successful; we have better health. We are happy!

The Good Book states: (Job 3.25) "For the thing which I greatly feared is come upon me, and that which I was afraid of is come unto me."

The only bad which can come from superstition is your belief in the omens. If you have faith that dire things will happen as a result of violating any of the rules of superstition,—you are then putting the laws of nature to work toward bringing about negative conditions. On the other hand, if you have faith in those omens which indicate good, then, too, you are putting the forces of nature to work,—but for good.

I said earlier that we are all subject to a certain number of breaks—some good—some bad. To the individual with a positive mind—bad breaks do not exist. To this fortunate person, everything which happens presents an opportunity. As you learned in Text 10 on ideas,—what might be a misfortune to one person is a definite opportunity to another.

A young lady had joyously looked forward to a certain "date" for several days. The time arrived and at the last moment, she learned that through unforeseen circumstances, her new friend could not keep his appointment. The usual thing would have been for this girl to mope and sigh the entire evening,—but she didn't. She realized that she was a bit behind with her reading and decided to spend the time improving her mind. In one of the articles she read, she gleaned an idea for a story which she wrote and sold, and later became very successful as a writer of short stories. What could have proved to be "bad luck" turned definitely to "good luck," not accidentally however,—but through the constructive mind of the girl.

A New York firm received an inquiry from Philadelphia. A salesman was assigned to it, who made a special trip to the Quaker City. This man worked on a straight commission basis—even paying his own travelling expenses. Upon arrival, he called on the man who had mailed the inquiry, fully expecting to meet a prospect whom he could sell, making a good commission for himself. To his dismay, it was found that the "prospect" was just a small boy who had written merely to receive a catalog with pictures he could cut out. This salesman could have done that which most humans would have done—"blow his top." But he didn't. He remembered that he, too, was a kid once, so with a sympathetic interest he talked to the boy about the pictures he would like to have and promised the lad that, upon his return to New York, he would mail a quantity of interesting pictures to him.

The promise was kept. The father of the boy was so impressed with the salesman—that on every opportunity he recommended this salesman with the result that what could have been a "wild goose chase" proved to be profitable indeed. This is another illustration where a positive mind helped a man to successfully convert unfavorable circumstances into big profit.

An unscrupulous land salesman induced an eastern family to sell their home and all of their belongings to buy acreage in Arizona, under the guise of fine farm land. This man, with his wife, arrived to find that the "farm" they bought was nothing but desert land with no vegetation other than cactus. Most people, under such circumstances, would go down for the count, feeling that they were completely sunk. This couple did not permit any such thing to happen. The husband had had a bad sinus condition and he noticed that in the warm dry air of Arizona his condition was much relieved;—cured in fact. The thought occurred to him that on his property he might be able to establish a sanatorium for respiratory ailments. He went back to his home city and interested a few friends in the enterprise—which proved profitable to him and highly beneficial to his patrons. Another reversal of "bad luck."

Your study of the **Magic Formula** will soon be completed. If you have been observant as you progressed from text to text, you will understand that the entire course is built with one purpose in mind;—to cause you to think in terms of "I CAN" instead of the negative "I CAN'T." You should know by now that when you can use the two words "I CAN" and really mean them—there is no limit as to what you might achieve.

This course could be given in just one short paragraph instead of 14 lessons. The paragraph could tell you that all you have to do is to **know** you can do things. But, such a course would be of little value. The significance of those words is so hard to comprehend that one must go through a well planned routine in order to make them a definite part of his consciousness.

If you have been fair to yourself throughout your study of the **Magic Formula,** right now you should be able to face yourself in the mirror and as you use the words "I CAN" feel the true meaning of them throughout every fiber of your being. No objective of any size should appear beyond you. You should be able to view the future with perfect poise, knowing that you are the master of your own destiny and that all roads are open to you, the choice of which road to take resting entirely with you.

If you have followed the suggested schedule, nearly thirteen weeks have elapsed since you started with Text 1. If you have applied all of the principles given, it is certain you have already had results far out of proportion to the very small investment you have made. And, no matter how many of your objectives have come into being, you have merely scratched the surface. Results will be accumulative. As you go on **day by day,** living these principles, your awareness of the power you possess will constantly increase, enabling you to reach heights of accomplishment heretofore undreamed of.

There is one great source of happiness which I have not touched on as yet. I left it until near the end so that you would be in a better position to take full advantage of it.

HAPPINESS COMES FROM GIVING HAPPINESS. As strange as it might seem, we have to have great wisdom before we can fully appreciate the truth of this statement. Hearing it usually brings to mind thoughts of doing without just so that we can help others. This, of course, is wrong. In saying that happiness comes from giving happiness, I am not approaching it in the light of charity. Very few people want charity any more than you want it. Giving happiness does not mean merely giving money to the poor. In fact, it does not often mean the giving of money at all. There are many, many things in life far more precious than money. In fact, it is frequently unwise to give money—or lend it. Instead of helping one to solve a problem, we are merely causing him to prolong his problems. The greatest help we can give anyone is to help him to help himself. But, this thought regarding happiness is not directed toward those who need help. There is an expression which sounds a bit cold, yet it is one which contains much truth. "Those who need help do not deserve it and those who deserve it, don't need it."

Gaining happiness by giving happiness is a subject which requires careful thought and reflection. Happiness is not a thing, it's a condition—a state of mind. You cannot buy happiness. You have it within and must give expression to it yourself,—otherwise you will not be happy.

The reason some of us are not happy is, because through certain barriers we are not giving forth that which we have within. Those barriers might be worry, fear, illness, lack, grief, etc. A feeling of insecurity will often hold one back from giving expression to happiness.

Literally speaking, we cannot give anyone happiness. But we can give reasons for giving **expression** to happiness,—and it is this condition I am now considering.

The motive which led me to the discoveries contained in this course, was my desire to pass on to others the opportunity of getting out of life the many blessings which, I had found, are available to all of us. Although there must be a commercial side to every venture, I am sincere when I say that my greatest reward has come from the letters I have received from those students who are now finding success and happiness through their study of Creative Psychology.

Now that you have acquired the keys unlocking the doors to greater success and better health, make yourself happier by helping others to gain happiness. Teach others to know they possess the same reservoir of power that you have discovered within yourself. Show them that they have the intelligence to enable them to climb and reach great heights.

There is a psychological advantage to be gained through helping others. The more you help the bigger and more important you become. The small person will resort to knocking and unpleasant gossip in the hopes of making others look small in comparison to himself. In reality, the more he knocks the smaller he makes himself. When you meet a person who has complimentary statements to say regarding everyone,— does that person look small in your eyes? To the contrary, you look at him as a genuinely big person.

So, seek every opportunity you have to help others to help themselves. Watch your circle of friends increase. Notice your personal power expanding. And,—best of all, you will be happy,—ideally so.

In the next and final text of your **Magic Formula,** you will be given a general review of the dominant ideas contained in all of the texts. Do not start on that review until you have thoroughly and fully digested this one.

You can prove conclusively that 13 is your lucky number, if you follow through with everything given in Text 13. Take at least a week on it,—and during the week make it a point to see how many times you can turn what appears to be a bad break into a good one. In other words, should something happen which could be considered as bad,—ask yourself: "How can I convert this incident into good?" You will be astonished and surprised to find how many blessings are coming to you in disguise.

And now,—*May Joy and Peace Be Yours!*

## InHABITing Pattern #25: A Practice
*Fire of Enthusiasm*
by Claude Bristol and Harold Sherman

You must keep in mind always that the intense fire of enthusiasm from within becomes a conflagration which affects all on your wave length as long as you radiate it. The vibrations you set up with your powerful rays of enthusiasm inspire others, raise them up, build and attract business . . . just as fear vibrations tap others down, repel and destroy.

It is an indisputable fact, irrespective of the times, that there is always business somewhere for the man who *believes* it exists and goes after it; but none for the person who is positive that none exists, and makes no endeavor to move.

Suggestion is one of the most powerful forces in the world. It has equal power in two directions—positive and negative—dependent on which direction you give it.

As a builder-upper, you can use suggestion upon yourself to excellent advantage. Now that you know the potency of thought, when you catch yourself taking on negative mental attitudes about anything you are doing or about the future, *stop everything!* Recognize at once the damage you are doing to yourself by permitting such thoughts to reside in your consciousness. Replace these wrong mental pictures with strong visual suggestions of the right kind. *See yourself* overcoming whatever difficulty you are facing, doing a better job, getting a better result tomorrow. Remember: the creative power within can only work on what you give it! A builder has to operate from a blueprint. If there are defects in the blueprint and he doesn't know about them, those defects will show up in the completed building. Unless you discover your wrong thinking, the wrong suggestions you are giving yourself each day, you'll attract what you are visualizing to you. Pass those suggestions on to your friends or associates and, if they accept them, they will help you produce the very conditions you have pictured!

Source: *TNT The Power Within You*. Claude M. Bristol and Harold Sherman. Prentice-Hall, Inc. New York. Pgs. 193-194. (1954)

## InHABITing Pattern #26: A Suggestion
*See Yourself As You Want To Be!*
by Claude Bristol and Harold Sherman

    Look in the mirror. Size yourself up. Are you the man or woman you want to be? If not, give yourself the suggestions that can help make you what you desire. See a mental picture of how you would like to appear to others, how you would like to express your personality. *Superimpose* this mental picture upon the actual image of yourself, before you! See the changes you must bring about in yourself, as though they had already occurred! *Repeat* this visualization day after day, night after night. Work at it! Remember the power of repetition, reiteration . . . tap, tap, tap!

    If others criticize you or don't believe you are capable of doing what you want to do . . . don't accept their suggestions! Analyze yourself to determine whether or not their criticisms are justified; and if they are, remove any resentment you may have had because of this criticism, give thanks that these defects were called to your attention, and get busy eliminating them so they will no longer hinder your upward progress. But maintain your belief in yourself! If you lose this, you lose everything. All success, big or small, starts with faith in self and faith in the creative power within. You must have it, and you must retain it—to go from where you are to where you want to be!

Say to yourself: "Each day I am going to improve and eventually I will remove the faults I discover in myself. Each day I am going to attain greater control of my mind and emotions. Each day I am going to overcome more of my fears and worries and other destructive thoughts. Each day I am developing greater health, happiness and prosperity. Each day I am going to find finer opportunities for serving others and the doing of worthwhile things. Each day . . . !"

Take it up from here. Create your own tomorrows by your own *positive suggestions* as applied to yourself and your needs.

Source: *TNT The Power Within You.* Claude M. Bristol and Harold Sherman. Prentice-Hall, Inc. New York. Pgs. 198-199. (1954)

# TEXT No. 14

# COURSE OVERVIEW AND SUMMARY

UNDER normal circumstances, when reaching the last of anything,—we think: "This is the end." This is not so with your **Magic Formula.** Ever since you started with Text 1 you have been gaining,—expanding, growing. Now we come to Text 14 which completes your course,—so far as printed material is concerned,—but **it is just the beginning** so far as your life is concerned. Yes, you have gained; more, perhaps than you might have originally expected; but the experience of being able to get what you really want in life is so new to you,—you would be an exception if you did any more than merely touch the possibilities offered through a real understanding of Creative Psychology.

Now, you **are** on your way. You know the statements made throughout the course are true. You know the future is of your own making and that you possess everything you need to enable you to climb to great heights.

As I write these lines, a picture comes to mind of a

day when I stood on the deck of a mighty steamer at a pier in New York. Every fiber in my being was vibrating with happy expectancy as I looked down upon the waving throng, watching the floating palace gracefully slip from the dock into the expansive blue. This picture came to mind as a symbol of how I see you, my beloved student, as you stand poised on the deck of life, gaily heading toward realities of your own choosing.

I am sincere in wanting the study of this **Magic Formula** to be the greatest adventure of your life. Knowing that, through it, you have reached new vistas of achievement and happiness means far more to me than the few pennies I might have made on the original sale of these texts to you. So let's pause for a few moments before we start our new life's journey and make certain we are getting the most out of each text given. The rest of this one will be devoted to pointing up a few of the high-lights; the dominants. But do not feel that upon closing this book you have drained it of its possibilities. If you were to read the texts through a dozen times you would gain something new each time you did so. Do you know why? Because as you develop, you add your thoughts to those given making them even more powerful.

You have accepted the thought that you should have your physical being examined at least once each year. You have your eyes examined about as often. You visit your dentist twice a year. Make it a habit to read through these 14 texts at least twice each year. This will keep all of these principles alive in your mind so your progress will be continuous.

**TEXT 1.** Determination was the dominant thought in Text 1. You were urged to build within yourself a determination so strong that nothing would hold you back from great achievement. Seven steps were given in making your initial start toward greater happiness and success, each one of them mighty important,—but **determination** is the most mighty suggestion of all contained in that text. This has been referred to throughout the course. By now you should know that nothing, absolutely nothing will deter you from getting out of life—**health, wealth** and **extreme happiness.**

Many long words in the fields of science are shortened by symbols and initials;—such as TNT meaning trinitrotoluol; HCN, DDT and many others. But, practically, all of these refer to substances which are on the destructive side. Let us be different and create a symbol which will stand for **good.** On the next page you will note a picture of the human eye over the letters DTN. Think of the eye as symbolical of the real "I" the mental self. Of course you already know what DTN symbolizes. Yes, **determination!** Why not fix this picture in your mind. See it so clearly that every time you see a picture of an eye, it will remind you of your determination to achieve big things in life. This symbol will also cause you to frequently check-up on yourself to make certain that you are living up to the promises you have made to yourself. Remember! Determination is your watchword.

**TEXT 2.** Perhaps when first reading Text 2, the real dominant thought did not appear as dominant to you. But now it has a new significance to you. To learn that **you are a mind with a body** instead of a body with a mind is an important key to your understanding that you are **master of your being.** In Text 2 are six affirmations, each one intended to produce a specific result. You cannot re-read anyone of them without gaining some good,—so do it often. Some students like to keep their texts by their beds and go to sleep with some positive thoughts in mind. This is an excellent idea and nothing but good can come from it. If you would try it, you would continue, I feel certain.

**TEXT 3.** The mind thinks in terms of pictures, the pictures are patterns and the patterns are accepted by the Creative Mind which proceeds to reproduce them in our beings and affairs.

In Text 3 you were put on a routine of self-discipline so far as your thoughts are concerned. You were warned that negative thoughts create negative reactions and were urged to go on a "mental diet" eliminating from your mind's menu every thought which leaned towards negative or destructive side.

You were asked to visualize an instrument with a magnetic needle which would register thought; leaning to the negative side when negative thoughts were accepted. Such an instrument (Thought-o-meter, we called it) would keep you alert and cause you to guide your thoughts toward the constructive side. It will be helpful to refer to Text 3, should you ever find yourself slipping—negatively.

**TEXT 4.** It takes courage to tell the public that the Magic Formula will help one to get what he wants out of life; success—possessions, better health—happiness. It takes courage because for the trivial cost of the course, the promised results appear to be so out of proportion. However, by the time you complete Text 4, you know this to be true. Right now, if you followed through on your different text, you are looking back on an array of objectives which have come into being as a result of your greater understanding of the powers you have within your Creative Mind. You also know that as yet you have just scratched the surface and that the realities of the past are little as compared to your expectations of the future. Whenever you have an unfulfilled desire—review Text 4.

**TEXT 5.** Hundreds of students have said that this text alone is worth many times the cost of the entire course. In fact the blessings it brings to you cannot be computed in terms of dollars and cents. Physical well-being cannot be evaluated with a dollar sign.

An exceptionally large percentage of bodily ills are caused by tenseness. A constant feeling of fatigue is probably one of the greatest penalties one pays for being tense. Of course, no one is tense through choice;—it is a bad physical habit one falls into. Act upon the thoughts and suggestions given in Text 5. And, if any of your loved ones are victims of constant tenseness, permit them to read this text so they will understand your enthusiasm for it.

**TEXT 6.** Can you stand before your mirror and with **determination** (DTN) say: "I am Master?" I once visited a man whose hobby was model railroads. He had a railroad system occupying several thousand square feet. It contained about a mile of track, mountains, cities, rivers, farms, everything in miniature.

This man could stand at a control panel and operate everything without leaving his seat. He could direct the trains to stop and start—to sidetrack while other trains passed, etc. The thrill he was getting from his hobby was apparent in his face which radiated happiness. What was the basis for this man's ecstasy? Perhaps he didn't realize it himself,—but **he was master.** He could stand there and cause everything to do as he wanted it to do.

No one, except those who have reached the point of self-mastery can realize the satisfaction which comes from knowing you are master of your own destiny and everything you are doing is of your own choice. You will bless Text 6 every time you see your self-mastery in action.

**TEXT 7.** You can date your entrance into that state known as success from the time you completed Text 7. Here you use a combination of your DTN and your self-mastery in taking yourself out of the wishing class into the realm of success. **You ARE a Success!**

Your enthusiasm for your Magic Formula is because, that through it, you are able to do your own achieving. The only satisfaction we get in life is through the things which we ourselves create. The Magic Formula has taught you that one actually works harder at being a failure than in being a success; and it also gives you the joy of seeing success come as a result of your own efforts.

**TEXT 8.** The **Magic Wand** as covered in this text is so important,—right now—before going further, close your eyes a moment and refer back to Text 8. Can you clearly see the Magic Wand? Do you fully understand it? Have you tried it? Nothing will seem beyond you after you become familiar with this unfailing principle.

The Magic Wand actually gives you the opportunity of seeing success principles in action.

You might hear many new words not familiar to you,—but until you begin to use those words, they do not belong to your vocabulary. The principle outlined in Text 8 does not become a part of you until you begin making use of it. Use it! Use it on big desires—and little ones. Once you fully appreciate the value of the Magic Wand, you'll prize it as one of the greatest gifts you gained from your Magic Formula.

**TEXT 9.** It is felt by many psychologists that at least one person out of every four is held back through timidity, worry, fear or some of the psychological complexes. What is covered in Text 2 regarding your being a mind with a body; coupled with the material in Text 6 on Self Mastery will make it comparatively simple for the student to dissolve his fears, his worries, his timidity, etc.

At one time in my own life I suffered severely from timidity. I was kept unhappy, not only because of what I missed in life, but due to my weakness in not being able to overcome the timidity. Most students lose their timidity before reaching Text 9;—practically all of them by the time they finish it.

Just as I suggested you share your text on relaxation with others,—do not hesitate doing the same with this one, especially where a loved one is being held back through this enemy of happiness.

**TEXT 10.** At this point I might repeat a motto I once wrote and which has been quoted many times throughout the United States. "A man may plod along for years without showing any signs of accomplishment....when sometime...unexpectedly...a powerful thought will seep into his mind—and a leader is born."

I feel certain that this very thing will happen to many of my students after they complete Text 10. Ideas are termed the spark plugs of success,—and they will begin sparking, once a person finds that his mind is just as fertile for constructive ideas as that of any other. Reviewing this text is always good for a substantial mental lift.

**TEXT 11.** Perhaps before you started this course you had never thought of yourself as a leader. Now, if you have followed all of the texts, step by step,—you nonchalantly take such a condition for granted.

You now have an entirely different concept of leadership than you probably had before. Most of us think of the leader as being dictatorial, dominating, even cruel. This is not leadership. A good leader is humble and even modest. A leader leads,—he does not drive.

Right now, it has been such a short time since you first read this text, it is probably very clear in your mind. Remember, however, that the principles covered in Text 11 are so valuable, you can well afford to review it occasionally.

TEXT 12. The gist of this entire text can be summed up in one simple sentence. **Gaining a good memory is merely a matter of developing a good memory consciousness.** Keep this thought in mind—always. Never see yourself in any other way except having a good memory. Should a fact slip from consciousness, know that it is because you let it slip and that you have the power to bring it back again. Do not, under any circumstances, make the mistake of feeling your memory is slipping. **You have a good memory.**

TEXT 13. "I have all kinds of luck, but it's all bad." This statement has been made many times and usually the one making the statement is right. He has gained a bad luck consciousness and without knowing it, is actually attracting bad luck to himself. This will never be true with you who have completed the **Magic Formula.** You know you are masters of your own destinies and if you are not heading in the direction you want to go,—you know that since you are at the

helm,—it is merely necessary to change your course. So now, let me say with all the sincerity I know....
*May Joy and Peace Be Yours!*

## InHABITing Pattern #27:  A Reading
### *Discontent*
### by Ella Wheeler Wilcox

Discontent.
*The splendid discontent of God*
  *With chaos made the world.*
*Set suns in place, and filled all space*
  *With stars that shone and whirled.*

*If apes had been content with tails,*
  *No thing of higher shape*
*Had come to birth:  the king of earth*
  *To-day would be an ape.*

*And from the discontent of man*
  *The world's best progress springs.*
*Then feed the flame (from God it came),*
  *Until you mount on wings.*

Source: *Poems of Power*. Ella Wheeler Wilcox. W.B. Conkey Company. Chicago. 1901. Pg. 48.

# InHABITing Pattern #28: A Meditation
## *Knock, Seek, Ask*
Gospel of Matthew: 7.7

**Jesus speaks:**
7 "Ask and it will be given to you; seek and you will find; knock and the door will be opened to you. 8 For everyone who asks receives; he who seeks finds; and to him who knocks, the door will be opened. 9 "Which of you, if his son asks for bread, will give him a stone? 10 Or if he asks for a fish, will give him a snake? 11 If you, then, though you are evil, know how to give good gifts to your children, how much more will your Father in heaven give good gifts to those who ask him? 12 So in everything, do to others what you would have them do to you, for this sums up the Law and the Prophets.

For additional information about Napoleon Hill products please contact the following locations:

**Napoleon Hill Foundation**
University of Virginia–Wise
College Relations Apt. C
1 College Avenue
Wise, VA 24293

Don Green, Executive Director
Annedia Sturgill, Executive Assistant

Telephone: 276-328-6700
email: napoleonhill@uvawise.edu

Website: www.naphill.org

www.ingramcontent.com/pod-product-compliance
Lightning Source LLC
Chambersburg PA
CBHW060515100426
42743CB00009B/1324